THE PHILOSOPHY OF
MAHATMA GANDHI

Some Other Works by
DHIRENDRA MOHAN DATTA

THE SIX WAYS OF KNOWING
AN INTRODUCTION TO INDIAN PHILOSOPHY
(in association with S. C. Chatterjee)
THE CHIEF CURRENTS OF CONTEMPORARY
PHILOSOPHY

→ THE PHILOSOPHY OF

Mahatma Gandhi

By Dhirendra Mohan Datta, *1898-*

THE UNIVERSITY OF WISCONSIN PRESS

Published 1953
The University of Wisconsin Press
Box 1379, Madison, Wisconsin 53701

The University of Wisconsin Press, Ltd.
70 Great Russell Street, London

Printings 1953, 1961, 1972

Printed in the United States of America
ISBN 0-299-01014-7, LC 53-9213

Changes in sources and references are incorporated in this printing following those made by the author in the Calcutta edition, 1968.

The publishers are grateful to Wallace Kirkland for permission to use the photograph of Gandhi on the front cover, and to T. Gelblum for that of the author on the back.

To My Wife
and
All women around the world
who work in obscurity
to help men work
in the limelight

Foreword

The rich treasure of Indian philosophical thought has been made available to English-speaking readers in many excellent translations. But it is a treasure of which few have availed themselves. The growing need for mutual understanding between East and West, however, emphasises the importance of study of this material. The time has come when it should find its place in the curricula of all our universities. And the best way, initially, to further this development is through the teaching of courses on our college campuses by visiting professors from India. It was considerations such as these that led to the visit of Professor D. M. Datta to America in the academic year 1951–52 to teach for the first semester at the University of Wisconsin and the balance of the year at the University of Minnesota. Two foundations helped to make this project possible. The Watumull Foundation of New York assisted the University of Minnesota, while the participation of the University of Wisconsin was made possible through funds of the Kemper K. Knapp bequest.

Indian philosophy could have found no better apostle to the West than Professor Datta. He wore the native Indian homespun cloth of a disciple of Gandhi, his obvious sincerity won the hearts of his students, as his careful and lucid expositions won their intellectual appreciation. Our thanks are due to India and, in particular, to the Government of the Province of Bihar, India, for having loaned him to us. At home Professor Datta is head of the Department of Philosophy at Patna College, Patna University, Patna, in Bihar.* He has won many distinctions in his professional career as philosopher and educator. He was a member of the East-West Philosophers' Conference held at the University of Hawaii. He is one of four scholars selected to edit a large two-volume work on the philosophy of East and West, which is being sponsored by the Government of India and will be published in England.† He is the author of numerous articles and of three important books, Six Ways of Knowing, Chief Currents of Contemporary Philosophy and, in association with S. C. Chatterjee, an Introduction to Indian Philosophy. These works reveal him as a distinguished member of that small coterie of scholars who are thoroughly at home in the history of ideas of both Europe and India.

As part of his duties as Kemper K. Knapp Visiting Professor Dr. Datta delivered several public lectures. The subject of the two most important of these was The Philosophy of Mahatma Gandhi. These lectures were broadcast several times on the radio and are of such value that Professor Datta was asked by the Kemper K. Knapp Committee to put them in form for publication. Gandhi himself has left us no systematic presentation of his philosophy. It has to be distilled from his autobiography, speeches and extensive writing on various subjects. For this difficult and important task Professor Datta is peculiarly well fitted, having been closely associated with Gandhi's movement for many years and be-

---

* He retired in 1953.

† Published since by G. Allen & Unwin, Ltd., London: History of Philosophy, Eastern and Western, Vol. I (1952), Vol. II (1953).

ing thoroughly familiar with both the Indian and Western backgrounds of Gandhi's thought. In these lectures, therefore, we have presented for the first time a concise, systematic, reliable, and reasonably full account of the philosophy which inspired and directed the life of a man who is not merely one of the most significant and influential figures of our age, but one of the small company of truly great leaders in history whose personalities have moved the spirit of multitudes to act with high devotion to a great cause.

A. Campbell Garnett

The University of Wisconsin
January, 1952

Preface

During 1922–25, just after finishing my studies at the University of Calcutta I took up constructive social work in East Bengal villages in response to Mahatma Gandhi's call to the educated youth of India. For a preliminary training I joined his home and training centre (ashrama) at Sabarmati (Bombay)*and enjoyed, for over six months, the unique privilege of living the life of work and worship which he initiated there. Though subsequently I came back to academic life in the cities, I have always drawn inspiration from the few years that I passed as one of the thousands of youths who tried to obey his call. Having had the advantage of reading his writings in Gujarati (his mother tongue), Hindi (the *lingua franca* of modern India) and English, and being also a student of philosophy, I had often felt an attraction for exploring the possibility of piecing together his scattered philosophical ideas and reducing them to a system, and judging also which of them could be traced back to ancient sources and which of them were his own. I am thankful to the University of Wisconsin, the Kemper Knapp Committee and especially its chairman, Professor Julian Harris, for providing me the opportunity for fulfilling the long-cherished desire.

I am thankful to Professor Gilbert H. Doane, the Librarian of the University of Wisconsin, his colleagues, and the Indian students of the University for cordial help and

* Now in Gujarat.

particularly for securing for me the necessary books from other libraries outside the state. Of the books of Gandhi on which I have more frequently drawn, the *Autobiography*, *Hindu Dharma*, *Anasakti-yoga* and the *Selections from Gandhi* (by Professor Nirmal Kumar Bose) are worth special mention. The Hindi collection of his letters under the title *Bapuke Ashirvad*, which was presented to me by the Principal, colleagues and students of Patna College (Patna, India) on the eve of my departure to America, was a constant source of inspiration.

I am especially grateful to Professor A. C. Garnett, Chairman of the Department of Philosophy, at the University of Wisconsin, who helped me at every stage of the work with his valuable advice and guidance, and to Professor Francis Shoemaker for many valuable suggestions. I am no less indebted to the students and teachers of the University who attended my courses during the fall semester of 1952 and helped me organize my ideas by constant discussion.

The audience of the public lectures raised, by their wonderful response to Gandhi's ideas, my drooping faith. This has greatly sustained me in this work of self-purifying literary labour.

Dhirendra Mohan Datta

University of Minnesota
March, 1952

Contents

xiii

mility and peace—Some moral maxims—The
cardinal virtues

Society: The natural classes—Dignity of labor—
Economic equality—Capital and labor—The
trusteeship of the rich—The ideal economic
organization of society—The menace of industrialism—The proper use of machines—Decentralization—Education—Men and women in society

Politics: Satyagraha as a political weapon—The
advantage of nonviolent fight—The genuine
few can léad—Political freedom—The state and
the individual—The spirit of true democracy—
Ideal government—Nationalism and internationalism

THE PHILOSOPHY OF
MAHATMA GANDHI

ABBREVIATIONS FOR REFERENCES IN FOOTNOTES

Autobiography M. K. Gandhi. *Gandhi's Autobiography: The Story of My Experiments with Truth.* Translated by Mahadev Desai. Ahmedabad: Navajivan Pub. House, 1948. American edition by the Public Affairs Press, Washington, D.C., 1948.

BMR N. K. Bose. Article reporting an interview with Gandhi, in *The Modern Review*, Calcutta, October, 1953.

BSG N. K. Bose, ed. *Selections from Gandhi.* Ahmedabad: Navajivan Pub. House, 1957.

FYM M. K. Gandhi. *From Yeravda Mandir.* (On Ashrama observances.) Ahmedabad: Navajivan Pub. House, 1957.

H *Harijan.*

HD M. K. Gandhi. *Hindu Dharma.* Edited by Bharatan Kumarappa. Ahmedabad: Navajivan Pub. House, 1958. (A collection of Gandhi's writings on Hinduism.)

YI *Young India.*

OTHER REFERENCES

Agarwal, Shriman Narayan. *The Gandhian Plan of Economic Development for India.* (Foreword by Mahatma Gandhi.) Bombay: Padma Publications, Ltd., 1944.

Fischer, Louis. *The Life of Mahatma Gandhi.* New York: Harper, 1950.

Jones, E. Stanley. *Mahatma Gandhi: An Interpretation.* New York: Abingdon-Cokesbury Press, 1948.

Radhakrishnan, Sarvepalli, ed. *Mahatma Gandhi: Essays and Reflections on His Life and Work, Presented to Him on His Seventieth Birthday, October 2nd, 1939.* 2d enl. ed. London: G. Allen & Unwin, Ltd., 1949.

Rolland, Romain. *Mahatma Gandhi: The Man Who Became One with the Universal Being.* Translated by Catherine D. Groth. New York and London: The Century Co., 1924.

Tähtinen, Unto. *Non-violence as an Ethical Principle.* Turku: Turun Yliopisto, 1964.

Varma, V. P. *The Political Philosophy of Gandhi and Sarvodaya.* Agra: L. N. Agarwal, 1965.

1

Background of Gandhi's Philosophy

> Children inherit the qualities of the parents, no less than their physical features. Environment does play an important part, but the original capital on which a child starts in life is inherited from its ancestors.—*Gandhi's Autobiography*, p. 381

To understand the philosophy of Mahatma Gandhi it is necessary to know certain things about the country and the family in which he was born, and his personal life which was passed in three continents—Asia, Europe, and Africa—yielding a variety of experiences which gradually shaped his ideas.

INDIA—ITS DIVERSITY AND UNITY

To many distant observers India seems a single geographical peninsula neatly bounded by the high mountains and the deep seas, which must, therefore, have a homogeneous population and culture; and its philosophy must, of course, always have been the world-negating Monistic Vedanta, as

3

so many western scholars of all times have testified. To most foreign travelers, on the other hand, India has appeared as a hopelessly heterogeneous medley of diverse peoples, tongues and creeds that defy consistency and baffle understanding. The truth—which can be perceived only by a patient and sympathetic observer who has the time to study the country closely—lies perhaps in the middle. India is a subtle unity beneath her apparent diversity.

Let us consider the diversity first. The physical features of India present the highest mountains of the world, capped by eternal snows in the north, low coasts in the south having eternal spring, and in addition, tracts of land lying in between having all kinds of altitudes and temperatures. Again, India has Cherapunji with the heaviest rainfall in the world, the fertile Gangetic valley, as well as the desert wastes of Rajputana and Sindh. During the nearly five thousand years of traceable history, India has been inhabited by the many aboriginals as well as by the diverse immigrant races which came in successive waves from the West and the East. "Racial types still occurring in the Indian population therefore contain . . . elements from all the main divisions of mankind not found elsewhere to the same extent," namely the Negrito, the Proto-Australoid, the Mongoloid, the Mediterranean, the western Brachycephals and the Nordic.[1] Naturally enough the cultures and languages of the people who came to settle in India also came with them and were added to the common stock. All the great religions of the world have originated in or come to India. What is now known as Hinduism arose more than four thousand years ago out of

1. See Biraja Sankar Guha, *Racial Elements of the Population* (Oxford Pamphlets on Indian Affairs No. 22, 1944), p. 2.

the vedic faith; the Vedas being the earliest Indo-European literature, perhaps partly developed in India, partly brought from outside by the Aryans who migrated into India from somewhere in Europe. During the sixth century B.C., Mahavira revived the non-vedic faith, now known as Jainism, and Gautama, the Buddha, founded Buddhism. Though nothing is known definitely about the original pre-vedic faith, it is supposed by some that the worship of Shiva and Shakti, to be found even now intermingled with other faiths, had a non-vedic aboriginal, perhaps Dravidian, origin. In later times the followers of early Christianity, the Jewish faith, and Zoroastrianism found asylum in India and they are still flourishing there. Since the eighth century A.D. successive batches of the followers of Mohammed attacked or conquered India and led to the establishment of his faith, Islam, which now commands a large following. From the fifteenth century onwards, with the successive advents of the Dutch, the French, and the British, the many later forms of Christianity came into India and established their churches.

The cultures and faiths during the last four thousand years inspired different types of philosophical systems, of which the principal ones would number about a dozen, and which present almost all the types of philosophy the world knows of. Atheism, polytheism, theism, and super-theism; scepticism, agnosticism, relativism, empiricism, and rationalism; subjectivism, indirect realism, and direct realism; materialism, dualism, and idealism; pluralism, monism, and indeterminism—have all had their votaries in different ages and parts of the country during these millenniums, and even the extant treatises—a fraction of the original total, most having been lost—amount to thousands. And the noteworthy thing about these systems and schools is that many of them have flourished side by side claiming allegiance from different temperaments.

But underlying these great diversities there have been many unifying influences which have been at work through the millenniums. Migration of communities to the less populated areas at different periods has conduced to some amount of mobility of the population. Intermarriage, where possible or favored, has led to the fusion of the many races and evolved a few general types of Indian features. Even where fusion has not been possible, the general tendency has been, not the elimination of one group by the other, but the formation of different classes as the limbs of one social organism. The idea of this organic social whole is even found in a hymn (the *Purusha-sukta*) of the *Rig Veda*. In different periods the conquest of the country or its major parts has brought the peoples under one rule. The spread of some strong religious movements in all parts and the establishment of places of pilgrimage in all quarters have fostered the growth of cultural unity. As religions and religious sects went on multiplying, attempts were made at successive stages to synthesize the diverse currents or to regard them as different alternative spiritual paths, any of which could be chosen according to one's aptitude. The *Brahma Sutra* and the *Bhagavad-Gita* in ancient times, the saints like Kabir, Nanak, Chaitanya in medieval times and those like Ramakrishna in modern times have repeatedly attempted synthesis and taught toleration.

Even in the sphere of philosophy, where the conflict of views regarding metaphysical questions became irreconcilable, scholars like Vijnana Bhikshu, Madhavacharya, and the

Jainas tried to systematize them either as a series of truths arrangeable in an ascending order of depth and subtlety or as different possible views of Reality. Moreover almost all the schools had a wonderful unity of moral outlook—the world being regarded as a moral stage, subject to moral laws that favor the conservation of moral values, human destiny being shaped by man's own action, and the highest good being attainable by knowledge, self-discipline, and selfless action.

EARLY LIFE OF GANDHI

In 1869 Mohandas Karamchand Gandhi was born in this land of complex traditions, in the small northwestern peninsula called Kathiawad, which forms one of the outlying parts of the Gujarati-speaking area of the province of Bombay.* His forebears belonged to the *Vaishya* (trading) class—the third of the four castes of Hinduism. But his father and grandfather preferred service as ministers in the native states of that province. They were both reputed as much for honest and loyal service as for their uncompromising sense of honor. His family followed the traditional theistic faith, called Vaishnavism, which inculcates the worship of God as the Supreme Person endowed with all auspicious qualities, and which rejects the belief in God as the Indeterminate Absolute transcending all assignable attributes. Devotion and self-surrender are the keynotes of this faith. Offering worship in the temples, taking sacred vows, and observing fasts on different holy days round the year, are the usual practices of the devout Vaishnavas. Gandhi was born and raised in such an atmosphere. His mother and his nurse were particu-

* Now in the state of Gujarat.

larly devout, and Gandhi imbibed their faith and learned the many current sacred names of God, particularly Rama, which he was taught to recite whenever in difficulty. But the locality had members of other faiths as well, such as the Jainas, Muslims, and Zoroastrians. Gandhi's father had friends among them, and when they visited, there were friendly discussions about those other faiths. Gandhi listened to them. He also read, as the *Autobiography* tells us, religious books in Gujarati from his father's library, such as the *Ramayana* (the life and story of Rama, the ideal and truthful Hindu King, adored also as an incarnation of God), the *Bhagavata* (a semi-historical and semi-allegorical devotional treatise which has been the chief source of inspiration to all theists in ancient and modern India), the *Manusmriti* (the ethical, social, and political laws of Manu, the law giver of ancient India). He thus had, as he says, some glimpses of religion even in early life. But in spite of an abundance of Christian literature, missionaries, and churches in India, Christianity failed to attract young Gandhi, as most other Hindu boys, whose feelings would be voiced by the following interesting explanation given by Gandhi in his *Autobiography:* "Only Christianity was at the time an exception. I developed a sort of dislike for it. And for a reason. In those days Christian missionaries used to stand in a corner near the high school and hold forth pouring abuses on Hindus and their gods."

As a boy, Gandhi was rather frail, nervous, and shy. He was none too brilliant in his studies. He mentions having read Gujarati, English, a little Sanskrit, of which he never felt very confident, and mathematics for his matriculation from the University of Bombay. But he was honest and laborious; and that helped him through the high school. He learned from his mother and neighbors the Indian maxim, "There is nothing higher than Truth." He also learned that harmlessness or nonviolence was the highest virtue (*ahimsa paramo dharmah*). Though this latter is universally acknowledged among the Hindus in all parts of India, it is most rigidly practised by the Vaishnavas and particularly the Jainas, the combined influence of which turned the native place of Gandhi, Gujarat, into the land of strictest vegetarianism. Gandhi grew in that atmosphere.

But the impact of Western ideas, which began to pour into India through the High Schools, Colleges, and Universities established by the British Government, had already begun to shake the agelong ideas and customs followed by Indians. The newly educated Indian minds began to rebel and break down, if not openly, at least secretly, some of these customs which, they thought, were the causes of their physical weakness and political slavery. Young Gandhi came for a time under the influence of some older students who secretly visited places where they could eat meat and smoke cigarettes tabooed at home. He even stole a few coppers and once some gold to meet such forbidden expenses. But soon he was seized by remorse and made a clean breast of his lapses to his father, gathering the moral courage to receive any punishment his father might inflict. But to his utter surprise his father forgave him with silent tears which completely washed away Gandhi's secret leanings. This was for him the first double lesson on the powers of truthfulness and love (*ahimsa*)—how truthfulness can arouse love, and love can silently, but most effectively, reform the heart. This sowed the seed of the twin principles of Truth and Love which grew larger and wider every day throughout his life. As Gandhi says in the *Autobiography:* "This was for me an object lesson in *Ahimsa.* . . . When such *Ahimsa* becomes all-embracing, it transforms everything it touches. There is no limit to its power." (p. 41)

As a Student in England

After the death of his father, his elder brother, a lawyer and head of their joint family, sent him to London in 1888 to study law. He could receive his mother's permission to go abroad only after taking before her the solemn vow to remain a strict vegetarian and to shun all evil company. This vow and the love and regard for his mother pulled him up from the brink of temptation and imminent fall on several occasions in London. The effect of this experience remained with him and made him take solemn vows on several occasions for making his pious wishes effective. He thus came to testify strongly, from his own life, the efficacy of taking solemn vows (*vrata*) as taught by the Hindu and Jaina scriptures.

It was in England that he diligently learned all the great and good things of the West. His legal studies did not demand much attention and he was free to pursue diverse paths of interest. He studied for the London matriculation to have a wide intellectual grounding—in Latin, French, English, as well as the elementary sciences. He tried even to take some lessons in dancing and music, though without much success. But he spent a large part of his time cultivating acquaintance through books, meetings, and personal discussions with the many moral, religious, and even dietetic movements of the West. It was also through Western appreciative exponents that he gained knowledge and confidence in the greatest things in Indian culture. Edwin Arnold's *The Light of Asia* gave him a touching impression of the life of Buddha and his English version of the *Bhagavad-Gita*, entitled *The Song Celestial*, converted him to the teachings of the *Gita*. He plodded through the Old Testament and read the New and was much impressed. He says:

But the New Testament produced a different impression, especially the *Sermon on the Mount* which went straight to my heart. I compared it with the *Gita*. The verses, "But I say unto you, that ye resist not evil: but whosoever shall smite thee on thy right cheek, turn to him the other also." . . . My young mind tried to unify the teaching of the *Gita*, the *Light of Asia* and the Sermon on the Mount. That renunciation was the highest form of religion appealed to me greatly. (*Autobiography*, p. 92)

Acquaintance with the theosophists and their literature introduced him to that religious movement for the unity of religions. From Carlyle's *Heroes and Hero-worship* he "learned of the Prophets' greatness, bravery and austere living." From his legal studies he learned two great things. First, the maxim that the two-thirds of law are facts. He applied this later in his legal as well as his political work. It fitted nicely into his respect for truth. He always tried to collect facts patiently and laboriously and let the accumulated strength of well-arranged and attested facts decide the case. The second legal principle that left an abiding impression on his mind is the idea of *trusteeship*, which he tried to apply later for the equal distribution of wealth by persuading the rich to realize that they were the trustees of the people's wealth and should voluntarily spend it for their welfare. During his sojourn in London he also cultivated the habit of spending very economically the money his brother sent him, and of keeping an accurate daily account of his expenditures —a habit that helped him to handle efficiently the public funds entrusted to him all through his long life.

On the whole it can be said that by the time he left London for India in 1891 after qualifying as a barrister-at-law (an attorney), all the basic principles of his life were set and habits accordingly formed. He became inclined toward a way of life which, he thought, was the best that the world had evolved through its greatest men and on which the East and the West could meet.

As a Lawyer, Social, and Political Worker in Africa

The later life of Gandhi in India, South Africa, and finally again in India may be regarded as the practical application of his earlier convictions in different fields and their extension in all directions of life.

After a short legal practice in India, without much success, he went to South Africa to prepare and conduct the case of an Indian Mohammedan merchant there. He toiled for months to collect all relevant facts, study law, and even bookkeeping, and by sheer devotion to truth he gained more knowledge about the case than even the two fighting businessmen themselves had, and he became master of the situation. He persuaded the parties to compromise the case and live in peace rather than ruin themselves by litigation. During the subsequent years—about twenty—he always followed the same principles in practice and, while his reputation and income as an honest lawyer increased, he espoused the cause of truth and righteousness and often made legal fights end in love. He saved both *his* soul and those of the litigants, and won the esteem of all.

In South Africa he came into closer contact with many good Christians, Quakers and others, and read more of Christianity. He was influenced also by some good Muslims and studied Islam. The theosophists, too, attracted him and helped him study more of Hinduism—works on the *Gita*, Vedanta, Yoga, Jainism, and the books of Swami Vivekananda (the disciple of Saint Ramakrishna) who preached very persuasively the ideas of Vedanta to the West and won high applause in America, Europe, and India. Raichand Bhai, a saintly Indian merchant, made a deep impression on him by his ideal Hindu life. He also studied the new interpretation of Christianity by Tolstoy and Ruskin, and its application by them in individual and social life. Referring to these influences in his *Autobiography* he says:

"Three moderns have left a deep impress on my life and captivated me: Raichand Bhai by his living contact; Tolstoy by his book, *The Kingdom of God Is Within You;* and Ruskin by his *Unto This Last.*" (p. 114)

It should be noted that Tolstoy's spiritual interpretation of Christianity, the presence of God within, brought Christianity near to the Vedantic idea of man; his emphasis on the Sermon on the Mount and the conquering of hatred by love and evil by nonresistance seemed to Gandhi to be in exact conformity with Buddhist and Jaina teachings about *Ahimsa* put into social practice. Tolstoy's book contained long letters and accounts of the practical application of the principle of nonresistance by Quakers and others in America who strengthened Tolstoy's convictions. Gandhi was thus influenced by those American Christians, too, indirectly through Tolstoy. But Gandhi was more directly influenced by the American moral reformer and writer Henry David Thoreau whose essay on "Civil Disobedience" he read with great admiration. It is interesting to note that Thoreau, a friend of Ralph Waldo Emerson, was himself influenced a good deal, like the latter, by the *Bhagavad-Gita* and the *Upanishads*.

From Ruskin's book Gandhi learned the dignity of manual labor, the idea that the good of the individual is contained in the good of all and that each can and should serve society by his own labor and profession in the field of his choice.

But all these lessons went side by side with a life of earnest practice into which by circumstances and inner leanings Gandhi came to be drawn. South Africa abounded in color prejudices, and even Gandhi, in spite of his British education, European dress and professional standing, was often subjected to all kinds of humiliation against which he revolted and protested only to provoke more insult and sometimes physical assault. Discriminative legislation also was proposed by the British rulers to debar Indians from rights of citizenship and other privileges. These circumstances offered to Gandhi the opportunities for applying the principles of conquering evil by love. He adopted passive or civil resistance by disobeying immoral laws, courting assault, imprisonment, and all kinds of suffering without retaliation or mental hatred and anger. He hoped that even the hardhearted rulers would ultimately be moved to pity and would realize their mistakes and rectify the wrongs. Gandhi was particularly hopeful about his method, for he had then the deep-rooted belief in the inner goodness of the British people which he thought could be aroused by moral appeal—by showing in an effective manner the genuineness of the grievances and the righteousness of the cause. And this method of nonviolent fight ultimately succeeded.

But behind this success lay his long personal preparation and training of the fellow-workers by his own life of sacrifice and firmness in the cause of truth and righteousness. He found that if he were to serve the society wholeheartedly and train workers, he must give up his greed for money, hankering for pleasures and lead a life of utter simplicity and self-control and teach others by his own example the possibility of such a life. This led him to all kinds of disciplines and experiments. He founded a rural farm and attracted similarly minded persons of different nationalities, white and nonwhite, to form a joint community based on the principle of plain living and high thinking. It was a big international family with a common kitchen, common ownership and run by the labor of each according to his or her capacity. In these long experiments in South Africa Gandhi worked in all conceivable and inconceivable capacities scarcely to be found in any *one* life before him. He worked as a school master, an accountant, an editor, a gardener, a barber, a tailor, a shoemaker, a compounder, a nurse, a midwife, a naturopathic physician, and what not. Several times while the British Government was involved in war he used his influence among Indians also to raise an ambulance corps, and led it himself to pick up the wounded and nurse them. Everywhere he passionately tried for perfection—both of the work and of himself. And selfless work widened his heart, deepened his convictions, increased the number of his followers and supporters, and ultimately his silent self-denial won the admiration of people all over the world who began to see that the high ideals of religion and morality were applicable even in political life.

As the Social and Political Leader of India

With this unique African experience Gandhi came back to India, after about twenty years, to place himself at the disposal of his native land. Many of his intimate co-workers came with him and he founded at Sabarmati (Gujarat) a farm and training center and named it Satyagraha Ashrama. His primary attention was to social service. He was determined to work for the removal of all social superstitions like untouchability, purda system, etc., to bring about unity between the Hindus and the Muslims, and to encourage the spread of cottage industries like spinning and weaving which could give employment to the vast majority of villagers who sat idle during some portion of the year. But gradually he was invited by the peasants, laborers, and others to solve *their* problems. He began to apply the method of truthfulness and love and to organize the people to make them nonviolent soldiers to win their righteous struggle against the British Government and the capitalists. By the increasing success of this method, Gandhi was gradually installed in the hearts of millions as their supreme leader.

He became fully convinced that the method which succeeded in the solution of smaller problems could also be successfully applied to the greatest problem of his country—

political slavery. But it could be applied only when the people could follow the path of truth and nonviolence. This demanded that they should first of all analyse themselves to find out their own defects which had made foreign rule possible. They should then purify themselves by removing their vices and should express their unanimous determination to be free. If the rulers still did not agree, all cooperation with the Government should be withdrawn by the people, which would automatically paralyze the Government, the machinery of which was ultimately run by the people. It was not, however, an easy method. Yet by repeated attempts through untold persecution and suffering Gandhi ultimately led India to freedom in 1947—thanks largely also to the moral pressure of the world at large, particularly of America, whose sympathy was roused by the high ideals and the nonviolent methods adopted by Gandhi.

For Gandhi the political freedom of India was not, however, the end, but only an important means. If India won freedom by the method of nonviolence, the method could be further extended for the solution of other problems in India and the world at large. So, though he was nearly eighty years old, he continued his mission of removing social evils and disharmony by his daily routine of work and worship until he was shot to death in 1948, ostensively for his love of peoples other than those of his community.

MRS. GANDHI

Even this brief account of Gandhi's life and experiments would be incomplete without some mention of his wife, Kasturbai Gandhi, who was always at his back like a shadow and, therefore, out of the limelight. She was his life's companion from the teens to the seventies. They grew together in body, mind, and spirit; worked together to raise their family of four sons, and their adopted "untouchable" girl; cooked and cleansed for their small family in earlier life, and for the bigger international family founded in South Africa and in India. She was the type of old Indian unobtrusive womanhood which claimed neither any separate existence nor any separate recognition. But yet, by complete self-effacement and identification with her husband, she enjoyed all the silent glory of a merged and united existence. She was with him in India and Africa, at home and in the community, in the kitchen as well as in prison. She followed all the zigzag path of trial and struggle through which Gandhi emerged from the narrower life of personal ambition to the wider life of love and service of God incarnate in downtrodden humanity. She also helped him gradually to transform love of the flesh into love of the spirit, and to concentrate all his energy on his social and political work.

It is important to add that Mrs. Gandhi, in spite of her submissive nature, also ruled and was often even feared. For example, when he was about to die of dysentery and no doctor could make him give up his self-chosen dietary restrictions, it was she who persuaded him even to break a vow and to take goat's milk which pulled him through.[2] As his American biographer Louis Fischer notes: "Gandhi feared neither man nor government, neither prison nor poverty nor

2. Shocked at the cruelty practised by some milkmen who tried to milk the last drop from cows and buffaloes, Gandhi had taken a vow of not drinking milk.

death. But he did fear his wife." It was again an example of the conquering power of self-effacing love.

The world never realized her quiet service and greatness until kind death liberated her soul from the burden of decaying flesh and she was found overnight reigning as "Ba"—the mother—in the heart of the nation—of India which Gandhi used to call his one big family. Millions of rupees flowed in spontaneously in response to an appeal to the nation for establishing Kastur Ba social service net-work throughout the country.

MAHATMA GANDHI

Tagore, the poet Nobel laureate of India and also one of the regenerators of modern India, accommodated in his campus at Santiniketan Gandhi's South African Party when it first came to India. He described Gandhi as "Mahatma (i.e. the Great Soul) in a beggar's garb." And the appellation of Mahatma stuck to him in spite of his bitter protest against it, when he saw later that it created in the people's mind the idea of him as a divine incarnation who could perform miracles and was able alone to take care of India's problems. Though he was the model of humility, he never believed in false humility. So we should fully accept what he said, again and again, namely that he was an ordinary human without any special prerogative or divine authority, neither a prophet nor a perfect being.

This is the most important fact for us, ordinary men and women. Unlike most of the greatest men of the world, Gandhi was not born great, but he made himself great, through struggle and experiment, with the help of two qualities, which every one of us can cultivate more and more, as Gandhi did, namely, *love of Truth* and *love of all fellow beings*. Gandhi can be a model and hope for all. His life shows that even an ordinary person has within him a capacity for increasing perfection that can work miracles, that is, things which would ordinarily be regarded as impossible.

In the light of this long life, which Gandhi rightly described as a series of experiments with truth, we can now try to understand his philosophy.

2

God, World, and Man

> I do not claim to have originated any new prin-
> ciple. I have simply tried in my own way to apply
> the eternal truths to our daily life and problems.
> . . . all my philosophy, if it may be called by
> that pretentious name, is contained in what I have
> said. You will not call it "Gandhism"; there is no
> "ism" about it. And no elaborate literature or prop-
> aganda is needed about it.—*Harijan*, March 28,
> 1936

The life of Gandhi briefly described in the prologue, and
his words quoted above, would make it clear that Gandhi
was not an originator of new ideas, nor could his ideas be
regarded as constituting a system of new philosophy in the
academic sense of the term. An academic philosophy to be
worthy of the title must first of all give new theories sup-
ported by arguments and even when the conclusions are old,
it must go through the arduous rational process of giving
new reasons in support of them and answer objections raised
against them. Gandhi had neither the special training nor the
inclination to undertake such a task. He learned what he
calls "the eternal truths" from the greatest traditional reli-

gious and philosophical teachers of the world. And only at times when confronted by doubts or opposition, did he try to justify them with argument.

But even then Gandhi selected and combined in his own way, out of the innumerable traditional teachings, those that appealed to him as sound and worthy of application to life. This led to a kind of new philosophical outlook, though the elements that went into its composition were old. It will be our endeavor in the present chapter and the next to find out the basic elements of that outlook, and present them under the usually accepted topics of philosophy, trying to set them into a coherent system, so far as possible.

GOD

The nuclear element of Gandhi's thought was his idea of God. All other elements ranged round this center in a peculiar way to form a new pattern. It will, therefore, be convenient to begin with it.

Though Gandhi's inquisitive mind tried to learn and assimilate the ideas of God from different sources, it only enriched the basic belief in divinity he had imbibed from the Vallabhist Vaishnava family in which he was born. The Vaishnavas are the most important section of the Theists, who form a large majority of the Hindus in modern India. They draw a part of their inspiration from the Vedas and the Upanishads and the Vedanta-sutra; but they do not accept the interpretation of these scriptures as given by the great Vedantist, Shankara, who upheld the doctrine of the Indeterminate Absolute (*Nirguna Brahman*). Four great Vaishnava teachers, Ramanuja, Nimbarka, Madhva, and

Vallabha, who succeeded Shankara, tried to refute his interpretation of God and all of them tried to establish the conception of God as a concrete person possessed of all auspicious qualities and perfections like omnipotence, omniscience, benevolence, and all-mercifulness. Whereas Shankara looked upon the world as a mere appearance resting on the ignorance of the individual (and therefore God's creatorship of the world also was for him no more real than the magician's creation of a show), all the Vaishnava teachers accepted the world and, therefore God's creatorship, as real. Again whereas Shankara regarded knowledge of God as the ultimate, attributeless reality as the path to liberation, all the Vaishnava teachers, on the contrary, agreed that liberation could be obtained only by the mercy of God propitiated by devotion and self-surrender. Naturally enough Shankara's abstract philosophical view remained confined mostly to a community of traditional followers in south India and a few highly intellectual scholars of the north; but Vaishnava Theism went on spreading among the masses throughout the country and from time to time acquired repeated impetus through the successive later generations of saints, devotees and poets. It was this Vaishnava Theism, which resembled Christianity and Mohammedanism, with which India came into contact, and which further influenced and strengthened the Indian theistic outlook. This made it very easy for Gandhi to accept the basic principles of theism in Christianity and other faiths of the world.

Gandhi was taught in early life to repeat also the name of Rama, regarded by some Vaishnavas as an Incarnation of God. He did not give it up even when he came to think that the name did not signify a historical person, the son of

Dasharatha. So he says (in an article in his paper *Harijan* of April 28, 1946): "My Rama . . . is not the historical Rama. . . . He is the eternal, the unborn, the one without a second. Him alone I worship." During the last few years of his life when he used to hold prayer meetings in the open, he used to sing a rhyme, which purported to hold that Rama, Ishvara, and Allah are all the names of God. And when he was shot at one such prayer meeting the last words on his lips were: "Rām, Rām!"

Among the other hymns which were sung by him along with the inmates of his Ashrama, every morning and evening, were those of the famous Vaishnava saints Tulsidas, Surdas, Mira Bai, and Narsingh Mehta (whose song describing the marks of a true Vaishnava was perhaps his most favorite), and also some theistic songs of Tagore, some Christian and Mohammedan hymns. It was this devout Theism of Gandhi's which swayed the hearts of millions of his compatriots of all faiths.

Again, though he was opposed to fatalism on the one hand, and was a firm believer in the theory that man can shape his destiny by his own action, on the other hand, he believed that man's perfection and liberation can come only by self-surrender and grace. So he says in his *Autobiography:* "For perfection or freedom from error comes only from grace. . . . Without an unreserved surrender to this grace, complete mastery over thought is impossible." This is typical of a Theist, a Vaishnava. Shankara and his orthodox followers, the Advaitins or monistic Vedantins, do not believe in grace, but in knowledge as the path to liberation.

When we consider these various points little doubt is left as to the fact that Gandhi was rather a Theist than an Advaitin; that is, he was not a follower of Shankara—a believer in an Indeterminate, Attributeless, Impersonal Absolute (*Nirguna Brahman*). Yet we are sometimes embarrassed by his occasional remarks which seem to go against this conclusion. The fact seems to be that he sometimes uses some of the Indian philosophical terms and turns of expressions which have passed into common parlance but lost their precise technical significance, of which he seems to be innocent.

In course of an article in his paper *Young India* (January 21, 1926), he says in reply to a friend's question:

I am an advaitist and yet I can support dvaitism (dualism). The world is changing every moment, and is therefore unreal, it has no permanent existence. But though it is constantly changing, it has a something about it which persists and it is therefore to that extent real. I have therefore no objection to calling it real and unreal, and thus being called an *anekantavadi* or *syadvadi*. But my syadvada is not the syadvada of the learned, it is peculiarly my own.

This paragraph shows, to an expert in Indian philosophy, that Gandhi is using the words *advaitist, dvaitism* and similarly *anekantavadi* and *syadvadi* without the precise knowledge of the meanings of those terms in technical philosophical discussions. But being aware that he is being dialectically driven beyond his depths he confesses, frankly enough, that he has been using words in his own sense, not like the learned. Space does not permit the full discursive analysis of this interesting paragraph. But suffice it to say that his own words clearly show that he is not the advaitist in the sense of a Shankarite who would neither support dualism nor the logic of Syadvada. On the contrary this very attempt to do justice to the unity and diversity of the world would strongly remind one of the theistic Vedantist, Nimbarka, who tries to reconcile Dvaita with Advaita. Nimbarka is the founder of one of the four schools of Vaishnava Theism. All these schools though rejecting the Advaita of Shankara, his monism that tolerates no plurality and change, advocate some kind of monism that tolerates them. It appears that Gandhi uses Advaita for this kind of monism.

Sometimes Gandhi speaks like the Shankarite, and calls the world unreal. But reading between the lines it is found that he perhaps means by the word "unreal" only "impermanent" or "transitory" (as in the paragraph cited above). His strong sense of duty towards suffering fellow beings stood in the way of his dismissing the world as wholly unreal. In *Harijan* (July 21, 1946) he writes: "Joy or what men call happiness may be, as it really is, a dream in a fleeting and transitory world. . . . But we cannot dismiss the suffering of our fellow creatures as unreal and thereby provide a moral alibi for ourselves. Even dreams are true while they last, and to the sufferer his suffering is a grim reality."

But it should be noted that even the non-Shankarite theists, though affirming, unlike Shankara, the reality of the world, attach to it a lower value and aesthetically describe it as a sport of God. Gandhi echoes this theistic sentiment when he says in *Young India* (March 5, 1925): "Let us dance to the tune of his Bansi-flute, and all would be well." In this connection he calls the world an illusion, Maya. But this word is also used by him, like the Vaishnavas, in the sense of Lila or sport. So he says: "Therefore, it is that Hinduism calls it all His sport—Lila, or calls it an illusion—Maya." It is taking this sportive view of God that he describes God as "the greatest tyrant . . . [who] . . . dashes the cup from our lips," . . . "to provide only mirth for Himself at our expense."

Again, though he sometimes says like a Shankarite that he does not believe in the personality of God, closer scrutiny shows that he means by the words the possibility of God's assuming the form of a human being. The following statement would make it clear:

"God is not a person. To affirm that He descends to earth every now and again in the form of a human being is a partial truth which merely signifies that such a person lives near to God." (*HD*, p. 131)

Even Western philosophers differ as to the exact meaning of personality. If personality implies self-consciousness plus will, Gandhi may be said to believe in the personality of God whom he regards as the omniscient, omnipotent creator, and just governor of the world. On the whole, therefore, it will be reasonable to think that Gandhi was a theist —a Vaishnava, rather than an Advaitist—a follower of Shankara.

It should be mentioned, however, that the Advaita school of Shankara received great attention in the West after the end of the last century, and it was this school, though with some modern adaptation, that the great Indian Vedantist, Vivekananda, preached and popularized in Europe and America. As a result of this it also regained some new prestige among the English-educated people in India. It is quite possible that Gandhi also was influenced by some of the more popular ideas of Advaita which passed current into the country. So we find him sometimes speaking in an Advaita language. But whatever might be the case these ideas floated loosely on his mind. His theistic attitude and outlook dominated his thoughts as well as his practical life.

God, for him, was the all-pervasive Reality, immanent in man and also in the world, which he regarded as His manifestation and creation. But unlike an ordinary pantheist he believed that God was also transcendent. He is in the world, as well as beyond it. He is not expressed fully by his creation —just as a poet is not by his poems. Gandhi has thus a comprehensive conception of God, like that of the western panentheists. Like Whitehead, in more recent times, who describes God from both the primordial and the consequent aspects and tries thereby to comprehend the diverse religious concepts of God, Gandhi also tries hard to comprehend the diverse elements of current religious traditions and to understand them as the different aspects of One Reality whose infinite richness surpasses our full comprehension. In the *Young India* article (January 21, 1926) he goes on to say:

I believe God to be creative as well as non-creative. . . . From the platform of the Jainas I prove the noncreative aspect of God, and from that of Ramanuja the creative aspect. As a matter of fact we are to know the Unknown, and this is why our speech falters, is inadequate and even often contradictory. That is why the *Vedas* describe *Brahman* as "not this, not this." But if He or It is not this, He or It *is*. . . . He is one and yet many; He is smaller than an atom, and yet bigger than the Himalayas.

The logic of the manifoldness of truth consequent on the many and inexhaustible possible aspects of Reality is particularly emphasized by the Jainas in India in their doctrines of *Syadvada* (that many apparently conflicting judgments are possible about any subject taken in different aspects and therefore each judgment gives only a partial truth), and *anekantavada* (that everything has multiple characters). Gandhi accepted this logic, for it enabled him to reconcile apparent contradictions in all fields of life and enabled him to have respect for others' views and humility about his own. We are not aware whether he had any knowledge of the technical arguments in support of the Jaina logic. He knew however the oftquoted Indian parable which favors this point of view. In the article previously mentioned he says:

> It has been my experience that I am always true from my point of view, and often wrong from the point of view of my honest critics. I know that we are both right from our respective points of view. And this knowledge saves me from attributing motives to my opponents or critics. The seven blind men who gave seven different descriptions of the elephant were all right from their respective points of view. I very much like this doctrine of the manyness of reality. It is this doctrine that has taught me to judge a Mussulman from his own standpoint and a Christian from his. Formerly I used to resent the ignorance of my opponents. Today I can love them because I am gifted with the eye to see myself as others see me and vice versa. I want to take the whole world in the embrace of my love. My anekantavada is the result of the twin doctrine of *satya* (i.e. truth) and *ahimsa* (i.e. love).

Gandhi found further confirmation of this all-inclusive attitude in the teachings of Jesus: "In my Father's house are many mansions"; "I am not come to destroy, but to fulfil." (John 14:2; Matthew 5:17)

It is with this catholic and all-round outlook that he described his conception of God on different occasions, from different points of view; and his basic idea of God as the all-pervasive reality underlying *all* phenomena, concrete and abstract, sometimes inspired him to ecstatic raptures that momentarily overflowed the well-disciplined measures of his habitual thought and speech. As one of the rare specimens of such a comprehensive and eloquent description we may take the following paragraph from *Young India* (March 5, 1925):

God is that indefinable something which we all feel but which we do not know. To me God is Truth and Love, God is Ethics and morality. God is fearlessness. God is the source of light and life and yet He is above and beyond all these. God is conscience. He is even the atheism of the atheist. He transcends speech and reason. He is a personal God to those who need His touch. He is the purest essence. He simply Is to those who have faith. He is long suffering. He is patient but He is also terrible. He is the greatest democrat the world knows, for he leaves us unfettered to make our own choice between evil and good. He is the greatest tyrant ever known for he often dashes the cup from our lips and under cover of free will leaves us a margin so wholly inadequate as to provide only mirth for himself at our expense. Therefore, it is that Hinduism calls all this sport—Lila, or calls it an illusion—Maya.

Students of philosophy may find in this description a very similar parallel to the famous description of God by the great scientific, mathematician-philosopher of the century, Alfred North Whitehead, in his *Process and Reality:*

"It is as true to say that God is permanent, and the world fluent, as that the world is permanent and God is fluent. It is as true to say that God is one and the world many, as that the world is one and God many." And so on.

The similarity between the two lies in their attempts to comprehend in one synthetic sweep the divergent aspects of Godhead and the different religious traditions representing different points of view. Both descriptions appear, to superficial view, as jumbles of contradictions. They can, however, be reconciled by recognizing the possibility of divergent aspects and viewpoints. Even Whitehead has been misunderstood and severely criticized by philosophers, and more so may be Gandhi. For they impose too great a strain on the customary moulds of thought. Yet, when the world is fast shrinking towards one community under the pressure of the scientific devices for overcoming space and time, and the peoples and ideas so long inhabiting isolated areas are running into one another, the necessity of synthetic outlooks is being more and more felt by the greatest men of the world in different spheres. It is no wonder, therefore, that Whiteheads and Gandhis would think alike.

God and Evil

In some respects, however, the paragraph cited above shows Gandhi moving too fast even for a Whitehead. For he takes our breath away when he stretches his idea of God not only to include the good and the benign aspects of the world, but even its terror, tyranny, and atheism. These points make us pause to understand what Gandhi really means by God.

In the history of the religions of the world we find two general types of conception about God. God is either conceived as a benign power struggling against an opposite principle or principles responsible for the world's evils, or God is regarded as the only and all-inclusive reality. Though in accordance with the first conception God may be, and often is, conceived as ultimately capable of overcoming the evils or Satan, yet it makes God subject to partial limitation by an opposite principle. The religious sentiment wants an all-perfect and all-complete object of worship as an unfailing source of help, and nothing but the second conception of God fully satisfies it. Moreover, religious belief is encouraged to posit the idea of an all-inclusive God by the monistic tendency of science which also tries, so far as possible, to explain the diverse phenomena of the world by bringing them under as few principles as possible, if not one principle. But as soon as God is made all-inclusive, evils also necessarily come to be lodged in Him. Developed Christianity and Monistic Indian thought with which Gandhi was in the deepest sympathy, face the problem of evil rather than sacrifice the infinity and sole reality of God. Trying to describe this all-inclusive idea of God, Gandhi is realistic enough to include His aspects of suffering, terror, and tyranny.

The question then naturally arises, does he then accept the position that God—this total reality—is both good and bad—as the above description seems to suggest? Or does he hold that the evil is only apparent, or that though it is real, it is or can be ultimately overcome? By family tradition and temperament Gandhi's heart remained captivated by the theistic romantic and benign conception of God as possessed of supreme grace, goodness, love, beauty, and harmony. The study of the great religions also strengthened this disposition. Throughout his long life of struggle he lived in such a God, courted His grace, took refuge in Him, "The Rock of Ages," prayed to Him, "Lead Kindly Light,"*saw Him in the great harmonies of nature and in man's love of man, and tried "to dance to the tune of His flute." But his rational mind and

* Cardinal Newman's hymn.

moral nature led him to recognize also the grim realities
of evils and imperfections in the world. They were, however, the greatest challenges to his theism. But his faith was
too great a source of practical value to him to be sacrificed.
He follows, therefore, the traditional ways of reconciling
the existence of evil with his belief in God as the only and
omnipotent and benevolent Reality. He tries to understand,
like Christian theists, moral evils, sins and vices, as being
due to the acts of man who has the freedom of will. To this
he sometimes adds the Indian theory of Karma according to
which actions of man are responsible not only for virtues
and vices, but also for the physical conditions into which he
is born. So Gandhi sometimes speaks of sins of men reacting
on nature and creating catastrophes.

He is sure that God could remove and prevent evils if He
would. But God like a good democrat allows man full opportunity to remove evils by his own free effort and thus
grow morally strong. As a stern and just educator God allows or directs by relentless laws the painful consequences
of man's action so that he may learn to correct himself. But
still, on the whole, he feels that the complete explanation of
evil could be given only if man were able to know fully the
motives of all actions of God. But that is not possible. So he
confesses (in *Young India* of October 11, 1928):

"I cannot account for the existence of evils by any rational
method. To want to do so is to be co-equal with God. I am
therefore humble enough to recognize evil as such. And I
call God long-suffering and patient precisely because He
permits evil in the world. I know that He has no evil."

He writes in another issue of that paper (March 5, 1925):

"He is the greatest democrat the world knows for he leaves us 'unfettered' to make our own choice between evil and good."

As a man is very unwilling to attribute bad motives to a tried friend and interprets even his apparently undesirable actions, of unknown motives, in the most charitable way and vaguely trusts that there must have been *some* good intention behind his curious behavior, similarly a person who has enjoyed repeatedly the benefits of the belief in God tries to understand the evils of the world as being inspired by some unknown good motive. The overwhelming force of the beneficial effects of faith in God enjoyed by him in life dispels from his mind both the doubts about God's existence and about His *bona fides*. Gandhi could not find it in his heart to believe that the evils that we find in the world are due to any evil intention of God who has been his unfailing friend throughout his life, in personal and public struggles.

God Is Truth, Truth Is God

Having thus overcome the obstacle of evil, Gandhi has little difficulty in conceiving God as the one, all-pervasive Reality in which everything—good and bad—lives, moves, and has its being. Even the atheism of the atheist appears to him to be a work of the Divine. Perhaps a short spell of atheism and scepticism which Gandhi experienced in early life convinced him of the healthy effect of rational doubt as a sound means to the generation of firm faith. Moreover, rational atheism appeared laudable as a fearless devotion to what the atheist regards as the truth. The spirit of the pursuit of truth is, therefore, common to both the rational theist and the rational atheist.

Gandhi finds here a valuable clue for the expansion of his faith and his notion of God. Writing in *Young India* (December 31, 1931) he says:

I would say with those who say God is Love, God is Love. But deep down in me I used to say that though God may be God, God is truth above all. . . . But two years ago, I went a step further and said Truth is God. . . . I then found that the nearest approach to truth was through love. But I also found that love has many meanings in the English language at least and that human love in the sense of passion could become a degrading thing also. I found, too, that love in the sense of *ahimsa* had only a limited number of votaries in the world. But I never found a double meaning in connection with truth and not even the atheists had demurred to the necessity or power of truth. But in their passion for discovering truth the atheists have not hesitated to deny the very existence of God—from their own point of view rightly. And it was because of this reason that I saw that rather than say God is Truth I should say *Truth is God.* (our italics)

This oft-quoted passage gives a glimpse into Gandhi's mind, the simple manner of its growth by experience and interaction, unhampered by the knowledge of philosophy which bristles with the different meanings of truth, distinctions between truth and reality, and the rules of formal logic which prevent the simple conversion of the proposition "God is Truth" into "Truth is God." A child gracefully describes movements with its supple limbs that the stiff adult frame fears to imitate. Poets, prophets, saints, and even the man in the street sometimes directly see relations and propound truths which science and philosophy can try to reach

only through long and arduous processes. Let us see, however, some of the chief difficulties which Gandhi's statements themselves would present to a student of philosophy.
Not to raise more difficulties than we can hope to settle in
this short treatise, we may accept the most common description of truth as conformity of knowledge with reality, and
let us also accept the common usage in English by which
true knowledge is also called a truth—just as a beautiful
woman is called a beauty. Yet how can we say of a being
or a reality like God that He is Truth, unless we ignore the
gulf that separates truth and reality? Truth is, after all, the
knowledge, the picture of reality in the human mind and
not reality itself, it will be said. But this difficulty is chiefly
caused by the assumption of the ordinary dualistic theory of
knowledge which is not accepted even by all philosophers.
As Professor J. H. Muirhead points out in the course of his
article on Gandhi (in *Mahatma Gandhi,* edited by S. Radhakrishnan), Plato, while thinking that in ordinary knowledge, through sense and imagination, knowledge and the
known remain distinct, holds that "There is a higher level
still . . . in which these two are united but also transcended
in a sense of an immediate vision and absorption in what is
seen." True knowledge or truth thus becomes identical with
reality. It is in the light of this highest knowledge that
prophets and seers identify truth with reality. As an example, Muirhead quotes the gospel saying, "Ye shall know the
truth, and the truth shall make you free."*This is also cited
by Tolstoy, at the very beginning of his book *The Kingdom
of God Is Within You,* which impressed Gandhi so much.
We may add that the Upanishads, which also influenced
Gandhi, describe God—Brahman—as Truth, Knowledge,

* John 8:32.

and Infinite. The Upanishadic seers—like the neo-platonic mystics of later days, the Sufis of Islam—and Tolstoy conceive of God as the reality within us, which directly manifests itself in our inner knowledge, consciousness, and life. So knowledge is nothing but God itself, and knowledge of God is not different from this God in us. Jesus also declares, according to St. John (14:6): "I am the way, and the truth, and the life."

It is by taking this inner view of God manifested in knowledge, love and conscience, and reason that Gandhi, like other spiritual thinkers and writers of the world, describes God as Truth, Love and Conscience, and even as atheism—the reason and faith that work within the atheist.[1]

Having thus understood Gandhi's description of God as Truth we may try to understand the validity of its converse, Truth is God. It is true that ordinarily such a simple conversion of a universal affirmative proposition would be fallacious. From "All men are mortal" we cannot deduce "All mortals are men." But there are exceptions to this rule too. When the subject and the predicate are equal in extent, simple conversion is permissible (e.g. "All men are rational animals" can be simply converted into "All rational animals are men"). Similarly the transition from "God is Truth" to "Truth is God" cannot be gainsaid by the rules of formal logic, since God is taken as identical with Truth.

Though the interchange of subject and predicate in an identical proposition is logically unimportant, it was a momentous psychological transition for Gandhi. He says in con-

1. For a modern inner view of God, in tune with the spirit of Tolstoy and Gandhi, see Arthur Campbell Garnett, *God in Us* (Chicago: Willet, Clark and Co., 1945).

tinuation of the passage cited above: "And I came to the conclusion after a continuous and relentless search after Truth
which began fifty years ago."

The psychological importance of the change is due to the
fact that the subject of a proposition or a sentence is "that
with which the speaker starts and about which he tries to
know and assert something." "God is Truth" reflects the
fact that Gandhi's search in life started with God, whom
he tried to know and describe, use and enjoy. As he says,
he accepted the idea of God from the world's existing religions. He seemed to have no doubt at the beginning about
the existence of God, about whom he was eager to know
more. But the world's unbelievers and atheists—with many
of whom he had to work in the political field—gradually
revealed to him that the traditional idea of God is subject
to very serious doubt. But he found that even they rejected
God, if at all, on honest enquiry, because they wanted truth,
without which the human reason could not be satisfied. Reason could reject everything but not truth. Truth has the
greatest appeal to all human beings. The hope of humanity
lies in organization based on appeal to reason, rather than
to blind religious notions about God which have wrought
havoc in the world. So he changed his emphasis from God
to Truth—which seemed to suggest: "I don't care for God
if He is anything but Truth, anything but the undeniable
Reality revealed in man and outside."

"Truth is God" also suggests: "Truth should be the object of worship." And it really was for Gandhi always. But
yet it waited to be known more clearly and needed emphatic
affirmation after experimentation. In practical consequence,
it was an expansion of his faith by which he could sympa-

thize as his brothers-in-faith with all persons who tried to follow, in their own lights, the common goal of Truth. This won for him—as a response to his real sympathy and love— the countless millions, including so-called atheists, who gathered around his social and political banner and marched after him braving bullets, prison, and death.

But let it not be forgotten that this was an *extension* of his early faith in God and not a relinquishing of anything that was vital in it. Narrow ideas of God have always created more mischief and hatred in the world than even honest atheism. In India, as well as in the Christian, Mohammedan, and other societies, persons not holding a particular conception of God have been criticized and hated as nastikas, atheists, heathens, kafirs, and the like. It is not remembered that "God," like "matter," may have a wide range of meanings for different persons with different experiences and backgrounds. A Newton, an Einstein, a Whitehead, a logical empiricist, and a man in the street, all believe in and speak of matter and use the common word. Yet their conceptions of matter vary widely. Similarly we can accept and recognize the widely diverse variations of the meaning of the word "God." Bishop Berkeley, while denying the ordinary belief in the extra-mental existence of matter, accepted it in the sense of a cluster of ideas. Even so the atheist who adores truth or a humanist who adores humanity or a naturalist who feels a cosmic emotion, though fighting shy of the word "God," may be said, in some senses, to accept God. Even they have their deities in the sense of the highest object of value, veneration, or love. And this would appear to be Gandhi's plea for the inclusion of the atheist within his religious fold. It was however a thin dilution of the faith which he prepared for sharing with all and sundry in his public life. There is little doubt that the faith he himself enjoyed, in prayer and silence, was much stronger. It was the "dynamo" behind his life of powerful activity.

PROOFS OF THE EXISTENCE OF GOD

Though Gandhi had no academic philosophical training, his study of religious books, particularly of Christian theology, and his earnest discussions on religious matters with all kinds of persons, made him well posted in most of the classical arguments for the existence of God. In the collection of his writings bearing on Hinduism and entitled *Hindu Dharma** an expert theologian can trace brief statements of the many arguments in his articles on God. The causal argument is present in the attempt: "If we exist, if our parents and their parents have existed, then it is proper to believe in the Parent of the whole creation." The cosmological and the teleological arguments are found blended together in: "There is orderliness in the universe, there is an unalterable law governing everything and every being that exists or lives. It is not a blind law; for no blind law can govern the conduct of living beings. . . . that law then which governs all life is God. Law and law-giver are one." The moral argument is very much valued by Gandhi and he constantly draws upon it. Conscience, for him, is the voice of God; the inner call to duty, to which he repeatedly turned and on which he waited by fast and vigil, was the direct intimation of the good and the divine in man. The authoritarian and the historical proofs appear together in: "Such testimony is to be found in the experiences of an unbroken line

* Sections 38–39.

of prophets and sages in all countries and climes." Gandhi sometimes takes advantage of the democratic criterion of majority, too, in testing the rightness of his faith when he says, humorously, for example, "I am one of the millions of wise men who believe in Him."

But in spite of all these arguments he knew, like Lotze and other philosophers, that no argument can convince a person unless there is some direct experience. "There is an indefinable mysterious Power that pervades everything. I feel it though I do not see it. It is this unseen Power which makes itself felt and yet defies all proof, because it is so unlike all that I perceive through my senses. It transcends the senses."

He recommends, therefore, also the pragmatic test:

He is no God who merely satisfies the intellect, if He ever does. God to be God must rule the heart and transform it. He must express Himself in every smallest act of His votary. . . .

He who would in his own person test the fact of God's presence can do so by a living faith. And since faith itself cannot be proved by extraneous evidence, the safest course is to believe in the moral government of the world and therefore in the supremacy of the moral law, the law of truth and love.*

It is by this practical method of acting on a working hypothesis so commonly employed in Science that Gandhi increased his faith day by day through his long life. Working like a scientist on the hypothesis that God—as Truth and Love—ruled the world, he behaved with love and trust toward all fellow beings in his private and political life. The response of love and trust which he obtained strengthened his faith, which in turn enabled him to retain love and trust, even for persons who appeared satanic to others. Even in very trying political situations which would drive others

* *YI*, October 11, 1928.

mad with anger and hatred, he never lost faith in the presence of God in man. Gandhi's repeated and unprecedented success generated faith also in his wavering colleagues and his opponents. Samuel Alexander, the British philosopher, points out that "It is our mental responses to objects that discover the objects to us." We can know the existence of the spirit in another person by the mind's response received from him. The same is true of the awareness of the existence of God. It is by the response to his faith that Gandhi came to strengthen his belief in God.

RELIGION

Though Gandhi was a lover of God, he had no attraction for any abstract entity called by that name. "God to be God must rule the heart and transform it." Religion means to accept God for life. Acceptance of God means to allow love, truth, and reason to rule the heart and remove selfishness, ill will, ignorance, and unreason, and all the passions like anger, greed, and lust that follow therefrom. Therefore, for him "the essence of religion is morality." . . . "True religion and true morality are inseparably bound up with each other." Yet, "Religion is to morality what water is to the seed that is sown in the soil." This simile would suggest that though morality is not impossible without religion, its growth is greatly helped by religion. But, on the other hand, morality helps religion by purifying the heart of passions and prejudices that stand in the way of realizing God in one's own self and in others. "The purer I try to become the nearer I feel to be to God." So religion and morality help each other.

"Prayer is the very soul and essence of religion," and

Gandhi prayed every morning and evening without fail, like, and with, the rising and the setting of the sun, wherever he was and whatever he did in his life, busier than which no life could be. But "Prayer is not asking. It is a longing of the soul. It is daily admission of one's weakness." [2] . . . "Our prayer is a heart search." It is "a call to self-purification" and "a call to humility." It is also an attempt to prepare ourselves "to share the sufferings of our fellows whoever they may be."

In all critical stages in his life, whenever he had to make a momentous decision, he would retire to himself, and even observe silence and fast, and check his accounts and motives with the God in him—Truth, Reason, and Love—and earnestly pray, "Lead kindly light." He came out refreshed, determined, and invigorated. He forged ahead, with redoubled energy and love, into outward action, enthusing his followers, winning the hearts of his opponents, and sweeping away, like a miracle, the age-long obstacles, hatred and shackles that degraded his countrymen and those that ruled over them. Repeated and increasing success confirmed his faith.

He tried to place his body and mind at the service of God, efface his ego and vanity by surrendering himself to God and doing His will and His work. He did not allow his little self and its narrow desires to stand in the way of the larger interest of humanity—which was God incarnate to him. So he often exclaimed impatiently, "I must reduce myself to zero." He tried to dedicate the results of his honest efforts—success as well as failure—to God, as the harvest of the Divine Will acting in him. He thus tried to escape the madden-

2. See *BSG*, p. 12.

ing vanity of success and the depressing effect of failure. But the harvest often pleased him and filled him with gratitude to the God in him and outside.

This was Gandhi's way of realizing God. For the philosophy of this way of life, or religion, he sought confirmation in the teachings of the great religious teachers, but particularly in the *Gita* which was his constant guide, on which he also wrote a commentary supporting in his own light the *Gita* doctrine of salvation through selfless action. In the introduction to this commentary he observes, "The Gita says: 'Do your allotted work but renounce its fruit—be detached and work—have no desire for reward and work,' " and "Salvation of the Gita is perfect peace."

Renunciation for Gandhi was not flying from the world, nor salvation a post-mortem goal. True renunciation is action without selfish motives and true salvation is liberation from the bondage of selfish desires and passions that fetter and torment man. Gandhi's final aim, like that of Christ, rightly interpreted, was "to bring heaven upon earth."

THE DIVERSE RELIGIONS

Gandhi's attitude towards the diverse historical religions of the earth may be briefly noted here. By his personal study of the many great religious scriptures he found that every one of them contained good precepts capable of helping man attain a truly religious life. But on the other hand he also found that the many interpretations, commentaries, and practices which have grown within each religious tradition contained things which were morally degrading and unsupportable by reason. So all religions were good as well as bad—good at the source and in ideals, bad in subsequent accretions and practices. Every person is, therefore, thrown back on his reason to select the good elements and reject the bad ones. Gandhi, therefore, places "sober reason" above the scriptures when they tend to confuse and mislead the mind.

Religion, therefore, becomes a personal quest and a way of life. Everyone should be free to choose his own. "Religion is a very personal matter," writes Gandhi in *Harijan* (December 28, 1936). "We should try by living the life according to our lights to share the best with one another, thus adding to the sum total of human effort to reach God."

On this basis he conceived the possibility of fellowship of all religions. He gives his considered opinion on this matter in the following statement:

> After long study and experience, I have come to the conclusion that (1) all religions are true; (2) all religions have some error in them; (3) all religions are almost as dear to me as my own Hinduism, in as much as all human beings should be as dear to one as one's own close relatives. My own veneration for other faiths is the same as that for my own faith; therefore, no thought of conversion is possible. The aim of the Fellowship should be to help a Hindu to become a better Hindu, a Mussalman to become a better Mussalman, and a Christian a better Christian. . . . Our prayer for others must be NOT "God, give him the light thou hast given me," BUT "Give him all the light and truth he needs for his development." Pray merely that your friends may become better men, whatever their form of religion.[3]

To the well-meaning Christian missionaries who were anxious to convert Indians to Christianity his request was: "Make us better Hindus, i.e. better men and women." A mere

---

3. *Ibid.*, pp. 258-59, from *Fellowship Report* (Report of a meeting of the Federation of International Fellowships, at Sabarmati, in January 1928).

change of name means little without a change of heart. The innumerable churches, denominations, quarrels, recriminations, and inquisitions, and color prejudices that checkered the history of Christianity held out no hopes to Gandhi. And the repeated wars that Christian nations waged against one another in modern times, and the parts played by the churches and their eminent bishops to help the decimation of their brothers in faith on the other side, made him sick unto death. He turned to the preacher to say: "It is better to allow our lives to speak for us than our words." [4]

He had unbounded veneration for all the great religious teachers. But they were to him Ideal Expressions of God. He did not attach, therefore, much importance to their historicity. So he thought of Rama, Krishna, as well as of Christ. He says:

> God did not bear the cross only 1900 years ago, but He bears it today, and He dies and is resurrected from day to day. It would be poor comfort to the world if it had to depend upon a historical God who died 2000 years ago. Do not then preach the God of history, but show Him as He lives today through you.[5]

An account of Gandhi's religious faith would be incomplete without a mention of his attitude towards Hinduism. The perusal of his writings on this topic collected and published under the title *Hindu Dharma* will throw full light on the matter. Gandhi believed that every individual is born with definite hereditary tendencies, in a cultural and physical environment and is, therefore, capable of development in a particular way. It is futile and unnecessary to ignore the

4. *YI*, August 11, 1927.
5. *Ibid.*

religious heritage with which an individual is born. The question is how to develop it to its best along its own easiest and quickest path. The words, symbols, and categories of the religion—the cross, the crescent, the om, heaven, hell, perdition, salvation, *moksha*, and the like—in the atmosphere in which a person is born, can arouse spiritual emotions and enthusiasm which no alien ones can so easily awaken. That is what he found in his own case, in spite of his closest association, and widest possible sympathies, with the followers of other religions. He found, therefore, that psychologically Hinduism would suit him best.

But did it suit him morally? Did he not hold: "Any tradition, however ancient, if inconsistent with morality, is fit to be banished from the land?" [6] In spite of the fact that he was painfully aware of the many evil practices and superstitions which had grown within Hinduism during the five thousand years of its development under diverse influences in different parts of the country, he felt sure that it was sound at its source and in its essentials which inculcated the highest ethical principles. The Upanishads, the *Gita* and the *Ramayana* of Tulsidas offered him the best nourishment for his rational mind and moral nature. The presence of God in all beings, the love of all creatures, the ethics of self-discipline, and selfless service, leading to liberation, were all present in them.

He doubted not that they were present in other religions too. But there was one more thing here, he missed elsewhere —the recognition of the value of other faiths, as taught for example, in the *Gita*. He was specially proud of this. For this

6. *Ibid.*, September 22, 1927.

enabled him to remain a Hindu and yet enjoy the beauties and benefits of other faiths and develop the most cordial relations to all human beings. He was proud too that the Hindus "gave shelter to the early Christians who had fled from persecution, also to the Jews known as Beni-Israel as also to the Parsis (Zoroastrians)." [7]

Hinduism, he thought, was a mighty ancient tree with many roots and branches and capable of unlimited development. Just as Protestants did not change their faith because of their dislike of Catholic practices, but they reformed Christianity, and just as the Unitarians did not also change their faith out of dislike for the doctrine of trinity, but reformed Christianity to their own liking, similarly, thought Gandhi, Hinduism could be reformed and has been reformed in all ages according to the best lights of the times. Fortunately Hinduism is not fettered by some fixed official creeds. "Hinduism is a living organism liable to growth and decay," and that was his great hope.

He felt that if he remained a true Hindu he could reform the Hindus in a more effective manner from within. Reformation of Hindu society in the teeth of all orthodox opposition was one of the chief tasks to which Gandhi dedicated his life; and no one could achieve so much in so short a time. That was also an achievement for humanity at large.

What the world needs today are good men who can pass the highest canons of every religion. The readiness with which Gandhi has been accepted by the best minds of all great faiths of the world as an example of their cherished

7. *HD*, p. 229.

ideals, shows that he passed such canons. He stands, therefore, above all faiths—yet so dear to many.

The Rock-bottom Unity

The secret of the appreciation of a really good man by
persons of all religions is that *behind all faiths there is a common ethical basis*—a universal religion. "It means," as he says,
"a belief in ordered moral government of the universe. . . .
This religion transcends Hinduism, Islam, Christianity, etc.
It does not supersede them. It harmonizes them and gives
them reality." [8] The "Study of other religions beside one's
own will give one a grasp of *the rock-bottom unity of all religions* and afford a glimpse also of the universal and absolute
truth which lies beyond the 'dust of creeds and faiths.' " [9]

THE WORLD

Gandhi's conception of the world of animate and inanimate nature follows from his conception of God. He does
not formulate it systematically in one place. We can get
glimpses into his mind from casual remarks in different con-
texts.

Nature's Charms

Nature for him is the outer expression of the all-pervasive living Reality. "God manifests Himself in innumerable
forms in this universe and every such manifestation com-

8. *BSG*, p. 256.   9. *YI*, December 6, 1928.

mands my spontaneous reverence." [10] One can find from this statement of Gandhi's his inner attitude towards nature. India is blessed with a rich variety of natural phenomena—the rolling clouds and the clear sky; the bright sun and the mellow moon, the visible stars and planets and the distant milky way; the six seasons turning round with their changing offerings of flowers, fruits, and luscious crops; rivers in spate, gurgling streams, and dreary sandy traces of dried up beds; lowly shrubs, twining creepers, and tall *sals* and banyans; birds of countless varieties, plumes, and voices; the innocent antelopes, the gorgeous peacocks, the royal Bengal tigers, and the mighty herds of elephants; the blue seas on three sides, the girdles of hills in the middle, and crowning all, the long and high Himalayas which stand in their mystic and solitary grandeur and invite the weary and the contemplative, but smile, with their eternal snows, at the childish attempts of the insolent to spoil nature. The greatest of the ancient and the modern Indian poets—Kalidasa and Tagore—observed, enjoyed, and responded to the diverse charms of nature and thereby won undying laurels at home and abroad. India's nature has attracted even some of her greatest modern scientists. Sir J. C. Bose's epoch-making researches about the sensitivity of plant life and Sir C. V. Raman's famous researches about the colors of the sky and the seas have drawn inspiration from that wonderful nature and opened up new vistas of knowledge. Religious aspirants of India have gone always back, for contemplation or for God, to the lap of nature—to the forests, the hills, or the banks of rivers and most of all to the Himalayas which combine all these features.

10. *Ibid.,* September 26, 1929.

Gandhi was quite sensitive to the charms of nature which he interpreted in his own way and responded to accordingly. He wanted to understand nature as an expression of God and tried to see life in everything, breaking down even the customary distinction between the animate and the inanimate. He drew inspiration for this view from Sir J. C. Bose's researches which he hoped would be more and more confirmed by science. The idea of the continuity through different forms of being got confirmation from the Darwinian theory of evolution which was one of the few modern scientific theories which seemed to have deeply influenced him. But the Darwinian theory was taken by him as supporting the idea of gradual progress—as it is popularly taken in the West too (contrary to the belief of some biologists). This confirmed his meliorism—the belief that man can improve his destiny if he will follow the path of nature.

RETURN TO NATURE

Gandhi's asceticism can even be interpreted to be a kind of wish to return to the lap of nature. His fondness for naturopathy, the treatment of diseases by the application of the major natural elements—water, earth, heat, light, and air—was an indication of this temper. He got inspiration in this matter from Just's *Return to Nature*. He was so confident of the healing power of nature that several times he staked the lives of his dearest ones and of himself in experimenting with nature's simple remedies even when the best modern medical treatment could be had for the mere consent. He loved to keep in touch with mother earth by taking long constitutionals barefooted and through open natural landscapes. His dress—the loin cloth—left the major parts of his well-formed body open to the healthy influences of light and air. This scanty linen interpreted also the ratio of his regard for social convention to his trust in nature. His physical habits seemed to declare: Nearer to nature, nearer to health; when the body is sick, go back to nature. One of his great hobbies throughout his life was to experiment with diet to find out "the natural diet of man."

But he turned to nature also for mental and spiritual health and repose. He said his prayers with his comrades in the open air under the canopy of starlit heavens before sunrise and at dusk. Once when he was nearly heart-broken owing to depressing political events, he felt the call of the Himalayas. But love of man stood in the way.

THE CONCEPTION OF BEAUTY

Perhaps from these facts we can find a clue to Gandhi's aesthetics [11] as well. Nearer to the God in nature and nearer to the God in man, the more of beauty. God expresses himself in the harmonies of nature which overcome discord and in the love and goodness of man which overcome hatred and evil. The harmonies of God enchant the soul. They are the source of beauty. Referring to the practice of tree-worship among some peoples in India, Gandhi once observed:

"I find in it a thing instinct with a deep pathos and poetic beauty. It symbolizes true reverence for the entire vegetable kingdom, which with its endless panorama of beautiful shapes

11. I am grateful to Professor Francis Shoemaker for drawing attention to the aesthetics of Gandhi.

and forms, declares to us as it were with a million tongues the greatness and glory of God." [12]

Again when he first visited some of the foothills of the Himalayas where Hindus go for pilgrimage he felt the same charm. He says in his *Autobiography:*

"I was charmed with the natural scenery . . . and bowed my head in reverence to our ancestors for their sense of the beautiful in nature, and for their foresight in investing beautiful manifestations of nature with religious significance."

The "panoramic scenes" of nature, "the starry heavens overhead stretching in an unending expanse," and the like, are for Gandhi more beautiful than human artistic products. They are "the eternal symbols of beauty" to him. This would imply that they also are not beautiful as such, but as symbolizing God, the original beauty. His favorite name of God, Rama, etymologically means "charming."

Among the products of human manufacture Gandhi saw beauty in those that involved honest labor, entailed no exploitation, reflected no greed, and served good purpose — in a word, those that expressed the God in man. By the habitual evaluation of human work in the light of his moral principles even his external senses could see beauty only in the good and ugliness in the bad. The spinning wheel, millions of which he introduced for employing the villagers fruitfully during their idle hours, became the very emblem of ideal social service. So the sound of the simple craft received from him the permanent epithet of "music of the wheel." On the other hand, the mills and machinery which disturbed the peaceful village industries, broke the homes,

12. *YI*, September 26, 1929.

created conflicts between capitalists and laborers, and were farther from nature, wore to him a hideous, dismal, and heartless look. No wonder his eyes should see in the smooth starchy texture of the mill cloth "a dead polish." On the contrary the handspun looked to him soft, lovely, and graceful. Its coarseness was crowded out of sight or perhaps was revealed as the very stuff of nature.

Coming more precisely to the "conscious art of man," like painting and music, we find naturally enough that he regards them as only the outer expressions of inner strivings of the soul and they are valuable in so far as they help man to self-realization. He says, "All true art is thus the expression of the soul. The outer forms have value only in so far as they are the expression of the inner spirit in man. . . . All true art must help the soul to realize its inner self." [13]

There is real beauty also in truth. "All truths, not merely true ideas, but truthful faces, truthful pictures or songs are highly beautiful. People generally fail to see beauty in truth." Moreover, "purity of life is the highest and truest art." [14]

We find thus that Gandhi's ideas of beauty, goodness, and truth run into one another. Because he traces each back to the concrete ultimate, God, in whom these three are blended together. God is true, good, and beautiful (*Satyam, Shivam,* and *Sundaram*). To understand the same fact from the subjective point of view Gandhi's mind strives after—and has attained in a considerable degree—a harmony and balance of all its diverse aspects, emotion, will, and thought. For such an integrated mind nothing is ultimately satisfactory to one side if it cannot satisfy the others. Or rather, such a

13. *BSG*, pp. 303 f.
14. *H*, February 19, 1938.

unified mind does not react piecemeal, but as a whole, and nothing that is not true, and good, and beautiful, can satisfy it. A picture that is judged beautiful by the isolated canons of beauty will jar on such a mind if it offends the moral sense or reason, that is the sense of consistency. Gandhi does not accept, therefore, "art for the sake of art." The production of a perfect art satisfying the whole and integrated mind is possible only for the all-round perfect artist. "True art must be evidence of happiness, contentment and purity of its authors." [15]

THE LAWS OF NATURE AND THE PLACE OF GOD

From the beauties of nature we may pass to another aspect which also impressed Gandhi very much. "All things in the universe including the sun and the moon and the stars, obey certain laws. Without the restraining influence of these laws the world would not go on for a single moment." [16] Gandhi perceives in the inexorable laws of nature nothing but the force and the will which maintains the world in harmony and order, and saves it from destruction. This force for him is nothing but God, and the laws are nothing but the ways of the working of that force. Therefore he thinks that there is ultimately no distinction between the law and the law-giver. "God's Law and God are not different things."

Though Gandhi, as a theist, was a believer in mercy, mercy did not mean for him God's willingness to exempt man from the operations of the law. Man has to take the consequences of his action. He believes in the Indian theory of *karma* or

15. *BSG*, p. 304.
16. *YI*, January 23, 1930.

action which inevitably generates its own results according to the laws which God laid down to rule the world justly. He says, "Whatever a man sows, that shall he reap. The law of Karma is inexorable and impossible of evasion. There is thus hardly any need for God to interfere. He laid down the law and, as it were, retired." [17]

Man and nature being both subject to the law of God, the acts of man influence nature and vice versa. Human sins bring automatic punishment. Criticizing some bad social customs he says: "I am superstitious enough to believe that all such sins that a nation commits react upon it physically. I believe that all these sins of ours have accumulated together to reduce us to a state of slavery." [18] In the great earthquake of Bihar he saw punishment for the moral sins of society.

But a person who cares to know the laws of God in nature with the help of the God in man, known as reason and love, and moulds his will and character in their light will enjoy the grace of God—the benefits of His laws. By living a life in accordance with nature he will enjoy health, safety, and prosperity; and by living in love with men and the living world he will get back love and sympathy. "Self-surrender" to the will of God would appear in this light nothing but obedient acceptance of the divine law of harmony, love, and reason. "Self-effacement" would mean effacement of the evil will that leads towards strife and disharmony (between man and nature, and man and his fellow beings), and towards unreason. Praying for Gandhi, as we already saw, was not "asking," but it was an ardent effort to acquire a constant remembrance of God (what the Indian theists

17. *Autobiography*, p. 298.
18. *YI*, September 15, 1927.

call *dhruva smriti*) so that life might be led in accordance with His laws. No perfection is possible without "mercy" and mercy is nothing but the saving grace of God as reason and love operating from within the head and the heart of man.

It will be realized thus that Gandhi's theism was not far from naturalism. Really speaking, strict naturalism—to be faithful to the spirit of truth and reason—is a theory of the head, indifferent to value and emotional valuation. But its theories touched up with the emotion, along lines indicated above, can convert, for the enjoyment of man, the vast *It* of nature into a *Thou*, as William James would put it. In Gandhi's well-balanced mind, emotion and will moved with knowledge and made him enjoy the fruits of his knowledge in every possible feeling, and both knowledge and feeling went into action in every sphere of life. This ideal of all-sided development is expressed in his writings: "But he is no God who merely satisfies the intellect, if he ever does. God to be God must rule the heart and transform it. He must express Himself in every smallest action of His votary."

To regard such a theistic version of naturalism as unscientific is to forget the limits of science, the province of science. Pure science is not concerned with the emotional evaluation and practical utilization of the truths discovered by it. If it is not unscientific to appreciate and applaud the vibrations of sound of particular timbres, volumes, and intensities as lovely music, and if it is not unscientific to love a complex configuration of electrons and protons as one's sweetheart rather than as a complex mathematical formula, then it is not also unscientific to *love* and *enjoy* nature, so wonderful in its constitution as discovered by science itself.

It is ultimately a matter of temperament and choice how best we should and can organize scientific ideas with emotion and action. Gandhi could sympathize with an honest atheist and could, on the other hand, say about the nature of God, "He is a personal God to those who need his touch." [19]

It must be pointed out that his own basic nature appreciated and longed for such a personal touch. He tried his utmost to assimilate the ordinary scientific ideas and tried to go a long way with naturalism. But where science was silent or stopped, his trusting mind did not. This was the region of his faith which gave him comfort and confidence. He realized that in spite of the attempt of science to understand nature, in the light of her laws, our knowledge was limited. There were many indescribable and inscrutable phenomena, and many uncertainties in our knowledge of the changeful phenomena of the world. In some of these he was inclined to see the hand of God and the play of His mercy. For example, several times he received money, unasked and from unknown sources, just when he was in great difficulty. Again, for twenty-five years he and the members of his several centers in South Africa and India had "uniform immunity" from snake-bite though there were snakes and they were not killed. Thinking retrospectively on such long and repeated experiences he observes in the *Autobiography:* "I see, with the eyes of faith, in this circumstance the hand of the God of Mercy." Apologetically he adds, "I have no other language to express the fact of the matter." He opines that such a thing "is not a fortuitous accident but a grace

19. *Ibid.*, March 5, 1925.

of God," and even if it be called a superstition he will "still hug that superstition." "Hug" is the word that correctly expresses his attitude of loving trust in God when reason fails to explain and yet does not permit the credulity of accepting the improbable as a matter of accident or chance coincidence.

"NATURE RED IN TOOTH AND CLAW"

Gandhi was not blind to the phenomena of destruction, discord, and death in the inanimate and animate world. He was aware of "nature red in tooth and claw." But looking back to the evolution of the world he felt convinced that the forces of attraction and love dominated over the opposite ones, and saved the planets and stars from clashing into destruction and also saved the animals from exterminating one another. Love acts even in the most ferocious animals which so tenderly nurse their young ones and makes their families possible. The gregarious instinct in insects, birds, and beasts shows again the unifying force of love and fellow-feeling. The progress of human society is a further expression of the same principle. "Nature lives by attraction. Mutual love enables Nature to persist." If man is to progress further he has to trust to this dominating and saving principle and organize society on its basis more and more.

Sometimes Gandhi tries even to go a step forward on the ground of his belief in the far-reaching consequences of human behavior on nature. Man's hatred calls forth hatred not only from man but also from other parts of nature. The whole world of nature is a field of mobile forces and a slight agitation somewhere shakes the entire world in perceptible and imperceptible ways—as Whitehead wanted to show. It was a belief like this which seemed once to prompt Gandhi to say that the snakes and the tigers are nature's or God's answers to man's anger and destructive tendencies. Perhaps he believed in the idea of the Yoga philosophy of India that if a man can totally overcome his inclination to harm others, then men and beasts will also shed all harmful propensities towards him. Love calls forth love from all. A good will generates goodness in all beings.

THE VAST WORLD OF SPACE AND TIME

Regarding Gandhi's conception of space and time we find that he was influenced by the general Indian ideas about them. The world is not believed, in Indian philosophy, to have originated at any assignable time. The cause of any event, as a Western logician and a scientist also will agree, is its immediate invariable antecedent (perhaps some would add to these adjectives "unconditional" too). So if we try to find out the cause of any event of the present world (or the totality of all such events which is the world itself) we would have to go back to the just previous antecedent or antecedents. If again we want the cause of the latter we have to go back to events just preceding it. If our curiosity still persists we can go back and back in time. We cannot stop at any stage as the first in time except arbitrarily, since regarding that, the question is also possible, what is the cause of that? So the very nature of the conception of time, as a series of succession, is such that we cannot possibly assign, nay, even think consistently of, the absolute beginning in time. The world is thus regarded as beginningless. Time is without beginning and without end.

This general Indian theory of time impresses many Indian
minds with the idea of infinite possibilities which, though
not actual now, might have been in the remote past or be
in the remote future. This generates again the tendency to
take a long-range view of things, rather than care for immediate success. A famous Sanskrit poet writes in the introduction to one of his early ventures: "Some day some one will
be born possessed of a similar mind (and appreciate my
poems). Time is without limit and the world is wide."*Time
did serve him well. In a similar manner, Gandhi hoped that
his ideals of nonviolence and truth would some day succeed.
So he retorted to a sceptical inquirer, "A few thousand years
are but a speck in the vast time circle."†We can find in it
one of the roots of his great patience, optimism, and far-
sight.

The infinite vastness of space and the universe is also a
dominant idea in the Indian mind. Our earth is only a part of
the planetary system which composes our world. But there
are many such worlds above and below. Sometimes they are
counted as fourteen. Religious poets and the Vaishnava theists derive from this a lesson for humility—how insignificant
is man compared with the earth, and how small the earth itself compared with the universe! Gandhi's constant striving
for humility was based on this realistic perception of the
tininess of the human body compared to the universe. But
with it, of course, he carried the counterbalancing idea of
the vast capacities of the spirit in man and the Vaishnava
idea that the human life is the greatest luck and opportunity:
"It is a rare thing to be born as a man."‡

* Bhavabhuti, in his *Malatimadhava.*
† *YI*, September 3, 1925.
‡ *Bhagavata*, 7.6.1; cf. *YI*, February 11, 1929. and *Autobiography*, p. 395.

MAN

Man is a complex being. His body is a part and product of nature and it grows and decays according to the laws of nature. The body is born of the parents and, therefore, "the original capital on which a child starts life is inherited from its ancestors," and the "environment does play an important part." But man is not all physical. Man has consciousness, reason, conscience, will, emotion, and similar qualities and powers which are the expressions of the spirit or soul present in him. But body and soul are not two ultimate and independent realities. The only ultimate reality is God who is manifested differently as body and as spirit, as matter and consciousness. Gandhi is not a dualist, but a monist who believes in one all-pervasive reality.

In the history of philosophy, in India and the West, there have been many philosophers, called dualists and pluralists, who have tried to understand and explain the world by assuming two or more ultimate and independent realities. But they have encountered the great problem as to how two or more absolutely different and independent entities could at all be interrelated if they are so different. Yet interrelation between mind and body is difficult to deny. To avoid this difficulty the monists try, in many different ways, to understand this universe by assuming one all-pervasive reality. There have been different types of monist in India, as in the West. Broadly speaking they are of two types. Shankara and his followers are the most uncompromising monists in India. They hold that all change and multiplicity are mere appearances. Therefore, according to them the body and the mind are the finite appearances of the One Ultimate Real, Brahman. So the self of man, correctly understood, is nothing but Brahman. The finitude of man is due to his ignorance of his real nature, which being known, man realizes his complete identity. This doctrine is known as *Advaita*, literally meaning nondualism. It is so called because it is the negative answer to the implied question: "Are man and God (Brahman) two?"

The other type of monism in India, while admitting the existence of One All-pervasive Reality, Brahman, or God, does not regard the finite and the multiple as mere appearances; the external objects, the bodies and selves are all *real* though finite. These monists try to explain the relation of the finite and the multiple realities to the One Reality in different ways, as we saw in an earlier section. All of them agree, however, to deny Shankara's doctrine that man and God—the self and Brahman—are absolutely identical in reality. These interpreters of the *Vedanta* are the founders of the many schools, commonly known as the Vaishnava schools and all are opposed to the *Advaita* of Shankara.

We have discussed previously that though Gandhi sometimes calls himself a follower of *Advaita*, he cannot be strictly regarded as following the *Advaita* of Shankara for he does not regard the world as a mere appearance. By *Advaita* he seemed to mean monism in general, including both the types distinguished above. This prestige term has sometimes been used in the wider sense of monism and he follows that trend.[20]

20. Even the position of Madhva, the strongest advocate of *Dvaita*, has been described as *Svatantra Advaita* by some recent followers; and Ramanuja's position is called *Vishishta-advaita*, Vallabha's *Shuddha-advaita*, and Nimbarka's *Dvaita-advaita*.

RELATION OF MAN TO GOD

Gandhi's conception of the relation of man to God shows again his general affinity to the Vaishnava thinkers rather than to Shankarites. He never enters into the intricacies of the exact relation between man and God; and it is not, therefore, possible to determine to which of the four leading Vaishnava schools, if any, he would belong. In his little commentary on the *Gita* he uses many concepts that characterize the general Vaishnava attitude which was inherited from the family and strengthened by the influence of Christianity and Islam. For example, again and again he speaks of God as master (*prabhu*) and the ideal man as the servant (*dasa*) of God. He also speaks of man as the part (*amsha*) of God or of the Divine Power. Sometimes again, he looks upon every man as the incarnation of God (*Jiv-matra ishvarke avatar hai*). But the most illuminating is his quotation of the current saying of Indian Mohammedans, which he cites here and in other writings with great approval: "Man is not God; but neither is he different from the light (or spark) of God (*adam khuda nahin; lekin khudake nurse adam juda nahin*)."

Here again we find his preference for some type of identity-in-difference relation which is differently maintained by the Vaishnava Vedantists and in recent times by Tagore. The Shankarites are advocates of rigid identity. Gandhi tries to keep his conception of man and God mobile and dynamic by thinking of God as force, as life, etc., as if to make him admit of divergent lines of manifestation, incarnation, and inspiration.

THE INDIVIDUAL

The individual is a real and unique center of the life of God and at the same time God is the one ground of all individuals and binds them together in an inseparable relation. So Gandhi says on the one hand, "The individual is the one supreme consideration." On the other hand, he says with great enthusiasm, "I believe in absolute oneness of God and *therefore also* of humanity. What though we have many bodies? We have but one soul. The rays of the sun are many through refraction. But they have the *same source*." [21]

We must pause here to understand clearly the old and modern Indian conceptions of individuality to make Gandhi's conception more intelligible. It has been much misunderstood; yet it has such a great importance for the conception of society and the state and man's duties towards them.

One great point to understand is that the Indian theists though admitting the existence of God as a creator never hold that the souls of individuals are created by God. Their souls are original and co-eternal with God, though parts of God and as such dependent on God. As creator God only wills into existence the different combinations of material elements, or God only differentiates and integrates the eternally existing matter, for the formation of the particular bodies and environmental objects for the souls. The souls— of human and subhuman living beings—are, therefore, eternal verities liable neither to creation nor to destruction. This is a very striking conception as compared with the theisms of other countries.

21. *BSG*, p. 25.

Even Shankara and his followers, who do not believe in the ultimate reality of separate human souls, affirm as strongly that *as we now are*, steeped in ignorance and the deep-rooted beliefs and habits resulting from it, we cannot gainsay our individualities which do exist for all practical purposes. We have to remove these, our ignorances, beliefs, and habits only by recognizing, utilizing, and employing our individualities—our bodies and minds—for gaining knowledge about ourselves and the world, for reforming gradually our bad emotions, passions, and habits by repeated contemplation of truths and action in their lights. The body, family, society, and state have all to be organized and utilized for the redemption of the individual from the fetters of ignorant ideas and habits and for the realization of his perfect unity with Brahman. The life of Shankara, spent in active social organization, illustrates his teaching.

The Buddhists who did not believe in any substance, therefore neither in God nor in the human soul, believed still the *fact* of personality created by ignorance and its many effects. And like the Shankarites they also recognized that it is not by ignoring personality but by its correct understanding and consequent reformation of feeling and will through action that one can realize the supra-personal state of nirvana. The long, active life of Buddha for the redemption of suffering fellow beings shows his compassion for all individuals.

In spite of the differences in the conception of the individual *all* Indian thinkers would, therefore, agree on the primary and practical importance of personality, its reorganization and utilization through a life of knowledge, discipline, and selfless activity—even if, for *some*, the ultimate goal is a supra-personal state.

It is true that the teachings of Buddha and Shankara were misunderstood and misapplied. The negative elements of their doctrines came to drown the positive and constructive elements. Similar things happened also in Christianity where the world-denying ascetic practices and institutions prevailed over the positive doctrines at times. There is no doctrine in the world which is too good to be corrupted.

But in recent times, during the last one hundred years, the positive aspects of the teachings of the old great philosophies of India have again been revived, in consonance with the modern Western emphasis. Vivekananda (1862–1902) has greatly emphasized the positive aspect of *Advaita Vedanta*, namely that "All this is nothing but Brahman," rather than the negative aspect of the same truth which stops short of the whole truth by saying "All this is nothing." On this basis, and following the good example of Christianity, he inculcated the idea "man-God" (*nar-narayana*), and the service of suffering humanity as the best worship of God and as the path to salvation. By infusing into the mind of man that he is nothing but Brahman, he inspired courage and confidence into the drooping spirit of the country which lost all self-confidence. He combined the compassion of Buddha, for the alleviation of the suffering of fellow beings, with the Advaita idea that there is but one Brahman in all, and final salvation cannot be attained until all are saved. The positive and dynamic results of this combination can be judged from his utterances like the following which whipped up the enthusiasm of the people for a renascence in all spheres of life: "A religion which will give us faith in ourselves, a national self-respect and the power to feed and educate the poor and relieve the misery around me. . . . If you want to find God, serve man." As Romain Rolland puts it: "And with this as his foundation stone, pride, ambition, love, faith, science and action, all his powers and all his desires were thrown into the mission of human service and united into one single flame."

Re-echoing the compassion of the Buddha as depicted in the Mahayana Buddhism (from which Chinese, Japanese, and Korean Buddhism have stemmed), Vivekananda solemnly declared like the Bodhi-sattva: "May I be born and reborn again and suffer a thousand miseries if I am able to worship *the only God* in whom I believe, *the sum total of all souls*, and above all my God, the wicked, my God the afflicted, my God the poor of all races." "Religion is not for empty bellies." [22]

The persuasive speeches and writings of Vivekananda ushered in the religious, national and yet international movements of India which culminated in her political freedom. His disciples have been working since throughout the country for the spread of education, social reformation, relief of the sick and the afflicted. They have also established many centers of *Vedanta* in America and Europe.

Tagore (1861–1941) taught, on the basis of the Upanishads, Buddhism, and the Vaishnava poets of medieval times, the same ideal of constructive social effort rather than a world-denying cult of defeatism; and he also attracted atten-

22. See Romain Rolland, *The Life of Vivekananda and the Universal Gospel*, trans. E. F. Malcolm-Smith (Mayavati, Almora, Himalayas: Advaita Ashrama, 1947), for these and similar ideas.

tion to the presence of God in the poor and the suffering people. In the *Gitanjali*,[23] which won the Nobel prize, he sings:

Here is thy footstool and there rest thy feet where live the poorest, and lowliest and lost.
He is there where the tiller is tilling the hard ground and where the path-maker is breaking stones. He is with them. . . . Put off thy holy mantle and even like him come down in the dusty soil.
Deliverance? Where is this deliverance to be found? Our master himself has joyfully taken upon him the bonds of creation; he is bound with us. . . . Meet him and stand by him in toil and in sweat of thy brow.

Personality for Tagore is "where infinite becomes finite without losing its infinity." It is the core of reality and value for man. In sympathy with Whitman he thinks about man that "in the centre of his world dwells his own personality." Man has to work from this center gradually to expand it towards infinity through love and service of man, love of nature and cultivation of all the creative arts. He founded an international university and social service center at Santiniketan (where Gandhi's party first lived in India) to give practical shape to his ideas. His song has become the national anthem of free India.

For understanding the ideological background of modern Indian life and the conception of man, it would be misleading to harp, therefore, on the traditional oversimplified notions of India and the East as the sleepy hollow of acosmism and defeatism, maya, neti neti, and nirvana and the like. These notions depict only antiquated half-truths which are some-

23. Rabindranath Tagore, *Gitanjali* (London: Macmillan & Co., Ltd., 1913), pp. 8–9.

times more misleading than ignorance and falsehood. They do not take into consideration the dynamic and constructive forces of ideology which helped the country rise from slavery through an intense and prolonged struggle for freedom against some of the mightiest forces of deep-rooted vested interests.

Gandhi utilized the new positive ideas of modern India by assimilating them in thought, living them in his life, and giving them social and political shapes. This entire concrete process and experience gave birth to his own philosophy of man and life that finally helped the people become free.

His notion of the presence of God in man amounts to a belief that man has free will, reason, conscience, and love. Man is the maker of his destiny. If he chooses to use his reason correctly and guides his life by listening to the dictates of his conscience (the inner voice of God), and lives with his fellow beings with love in his heart, he can realize God and bring heaven on earth.

Every individual is unique because of his peculiar physical and mental inheritance and equipment. What an individual now is, is the effect of his action—his habits of thinking, feeling, speaking, and acting in the past. Man makes himself through all these diverse activities, internal and external. They appear to be so insignificant separately, but taken together they create the tremendous forces that shape his health, character, and his entire destiny. "Man is the maker of his destiny." But he must thoroughly understand his peculiar nature and try to perfect it. He can degrade himself by ignoring truth, neglecting conscience, and pandering to the animal passions, and can turn himself into a brute. But he can, if he will, also follow an opposite path and become more and more like God, in love, goodness, and abiding joy, for "The divine powers within us are infinite." By his life and teachings Gandhi exhorts like the *Gita:* "Raise yourself by yourself; do not depress yourself. You are your friend, you are your own foe." So also taught Buddha: "Be a light unto thyself." This is also the purport of the teaching of Jesus in the parable of the talents.

What has raised man to the present state above the brutish life is control of the bad impulses. "The brute by nature knows no self-restraint. Man is man because he is capable of, and only in so far as he exercises, self-restraint," says Gandhi in his *Autobiography* (p. 387). Human civilization has become possible because of the control of the baser tendencies like hatred and selfishness, and it can flourish in so far as these are replaced by good-will and love.

THE PROGRESS OF MAN

When Gandhi is in a mood to philosophize on the course of history he takes a long-sighted view and judges things as a whole in the light of the dominant trends. Viewing human history in this way he feels confident that humanity is on the whole progressing. He says, therefore, "I believe that the sum total of the energy of mankind is not to bring us down but to lift us up, and that is the result of the definite, if unconscious, working of the law of love." [24]

But though it means, for him, that God, as love and reason, is working through man to help man raise himself, he does not forget that God has given man freedom to play the game in his own way, only trusting that man would learn to improve himself even by his failures, making them the pillars of his success. So Gandhi speaks in a balanced tone:

24. *YI*, November 12, 1931.

If we believe that mankind has steadily progressed towards *ahimsa* (i.e. love), it follows that it has to progress towards it still further. Nothing in this world is static, everything is kinetic. If there is no progression, then there is inevitable retrogression. No one can remain without the eternal cycle, unless it be God Himself.[25]

To follow the path of progress man must constantly strive to improve his life by improving his morals, society, and politics. We shall consider these topics in the next chapter to see how Gandhi applied his philosophy to his own life and to practical social and political service.

25. *H*, August 11, 1940.

3

Morals, Society, and Politics

> But this is Philosophy. Let me pray and let my
> readers join in the prayer to God that he may give
> me the strength to live up to that philosophy. For
> philosophy without life corresponding is a body
> without life.—*Young India*, April 14, 1927
> I claim that human mind or human society is
> not divided into watertight compartments called
> social, political and religious. All act and react
> upon one another.—*Young India*, March 2, 1922

Gandhi's philosophy of morals, society, and politics would
seem to be only an application of his philosophy of God,
nature, and man. It would, however, be more true to say that
both of these philosophies grew simultaneously in and out
of a life of varied experience in which thought, feeling, and
action worked together in harmony.

Man's ultimate aim is the realization of God, and all his activities, social, political, religious, have to be guided by the ultimate
aim of the vision of God. The immediate service of all human
beings becomes a necessary part of the endeavour, simply because the only way to find God is to see Him in His creation and
be one with it. This can only be done by service of all.[1]

1. *BSG*, p. 25.

73

This is an expression of the positive spirit of seeking God through the service of man, the realization of the truth through action. We have seen how this spirit grew in modern India and paved the way for a renascence, by the reinterpretation of ancient Indian thought and redistribution of emphasis. But the renascence which started on the level of thought and feeling and only partially in social action, attained in Gandhi the width and the intensity of a flood that burst into all-sided activity, private, social, and political.

It is important to bear in mind that the influence of the West contributed to the strength of this new movement in India in two ways. First, the impact of the West on India through British rule was the stimulating cause of the cultural renascence in the country before the appearance of Gandhi. Secondly, Gandhi himself was directly influenced by Western Christian social and political reformers like Tolstoy, Ruskin, Thoreau, and the Friends (Quakers) of Great Britain, America, and Africa. But for this second influence India's path of social, economic, and political recovery would have been in many respects more or less a blind imitation of the West. These Western critics and reformers of Christianity and of the economic and the political ideologies of the West showed Gandhi the dangers of the blind imitation of the West. Tolstoy's book called *The Kingdom of God Is Within You or, Christianity Not as a Mystical Teaching but as a New Concept of Life* gave him the idea of the possibility of the application of the high principles of love and nonresistance in practical politics. These Western ideas only confirmed what Gandhi learned also from the best of Indian teachers.

MORALITY

Morality is, for Gandhi, the very foundation of life. The existence and progress of individuals and society depend on morality. It keeps in check the passions and impulses that lead to discord, strife, and ruin, and it promotes the other-regarding feelings that create harmony, peace, and happiness. Morality has the greatest survival value. It has evolved gradually through the long process of the evolution of man. It has been found more and more helpful and has come to be ingrained in his very nature. The moral sense or conscience has, therefore, become man's inner guide.

The realization of God is the ultimate goal of human life. But God is not an abstract entity. He is the Truth or Reality that lives in man's own self and in the selves of others. He is, of course, the reality in every thing in the universe. But He is manifested in the living more clearly than in the nonliving, and in man more than in the other living beings. The realization of God can, therefore, be attained best through the realization of the God in one's own self and in humanity.

Every individual is a definite center of the life of God manifested through particular physical and mental conditions. Everyone is born with certain definite tendencies, good and bad, selfish and unselfish. He must try to know himself and reform himself, and gradually widen his limited circle of existence towards the Infinite Self, God. This can be done only by considering and including the interests of others. The path to the realization of the True Self or God, therefore, lies through the love of others and the performance of duties towards others as such love demands. Morality thus becomes "the essence of religion."

LOVE

Love (*ahimsa*) is the essence of morality. It is the nearest approach to God, the Truth manifested in our knowledge of Reality. Love helps the finite individual to widen his narrow self. It breaks the barrier between himself and others and makes the life of the individual include more and more of others, and it takes him thus towards the Universal or God. Love in man is the Divine Law or God inherent in him. Without this Divine Impulse man would have remained confined to his narrow ambit of selfish existence, if he could exist at all. No amount of reasoning or threat can accomplish what love can do quite spontaneously. All duties towards one's fellow beings follow from love. The performance of duty is also made pleasant by love. Love penetrates into every sphere of life and tunes all impulses to one pleasant, orchestral harmony. Gandhi tried to realize this truth. So he says:

"My life is one indivisible whole and all activities run into one another, and they all have their rise in my insatiable love of mankind."

Again, "For me, the Law of complete Love is the Law of my being." [2]

KNOWLEDGE

But love itself has to be gradually perfected by knowledge and moral effort. Love in its unenlightened form is manifest as a blind animal appetite centered mostly in the body. Knowledge liberates love from its narrow limits. When man

2. *Ibid.*, p. 44.

is ignorant of his real nature, he is moved by the cravings of the flesh with which he completely identifies himself. But when he realizes his underlying Reality and through it his inseparable relations with the rest of existence, his love extends beyond his body and its immediate interests. Thus we find that love and knowledge of Truth help each other. Love without Truth would be blind and narrow, Truth without love would be a mere unrealized Ideal.

Gandhi places, therefore, great emphasis on the necessity of knowledge for morality. Mere mechanical action per-formed either under the influence of blind impulse or customs is not really moral. Morality implies conscious, deliberate volition.

No action, which is not voluntary can be called moral. So long as we act like machines, there can be no question of moral-ity. If we want to call an action moral, it should have been done consciously and as a matter of duty. Any action that is dictated by fear or by coercion of any kind ceases to be moral.[3]

A good action requires also the knowledge of the conditions of other fellow beings concerned, the environmental conditions and particularly the motives behind the action. Self-analysis, therefore, acquires a great importance in the ethics of Gandhi. One must always be on guard, he thinks, and watch the motives that prompt one's action. "Our desires and motives may be divided into two classes—selfish and unselfish. All selfish desires are immoral, while the desire to improve ourselves for the sake of doing good to others is truly moral." [4] Self-analysis is necessary to check our selfish motives. Without self-analysis there cannot be self-purifica-

3. *Ibid.*, p. 254.
4. *Ibid.*, p. 255.

tion. Whenever Gandhi had any conflict or discord with individuals or any organizations his first step was to retire into himself to check his motives and actions; and if he found any defect on his side he would confess it and try to remove it.

But like some modern psychologists Gandhi was aware that self-analysis might be sometimes deceptive and that others could at times see our motives and desires more clearly by observing our behavior. So he also attached importance to the opinion of others. His advice was: "We must also try to see as others see us."

We find thus that knowledge, from every point of view, is essential for good, as well as successful, moral life.

Free Will

Freedom of will is a necessary postulate of morality, according to Gandhi, as to most ethical thinkers. But he recognizes that man is not entirely free. Every man is born with certain limitations. He should know them and develop himself to the best of his capacities. All limitations cannot be totally overcome. Moreover, the laws of nature to which man is subject prescribe also some limits. But man can know these laws and learn to obey them and derive benefits from them. Man's own action, too, creates habits and tendencies; and he is driven by them too. The tendencies with which man is born are regarded by Gandhi, like ancient Indian philosophers, as also the effects of his own action in previous lives. But in spite of all these limiting influences, and even within their arena, man has sufficient scope for exerting his will and moulding his environment, body, and mind. He can thus improve his conditions and change his habits and shape his destiny.

SOUL FORCE

But he can draw additional strength from another source too if he has the will and the faith. One of the chief sources of the weakness and helplessness of man is his egotism—his mental identification of himself with his mind and body. This isolates himself from the rest of Reality. To superficial thought the ego appears as the very source of energy, and the assertion of the ego appears to be the only way of getting power and success. This is, however, a partial truth. Self-assertion is necessary and even beneficial for a person who suffers from utter inertia (*tamas*) and who cannot even command the physical and mental energy normally available to him. But one who has not only perfectly mastered his body and mind but has also realized that he is an inseparable part of the All-pervasive, Omnipotent Reality, can command an extraordinary power, particularly for the service of humanity.[5] Such a person has a much greater confidence in himself and others as parts of the one whole. He has an ardent love for others by which he can serve, move, and lead his fellow beings towards perfection with an ever-increasing speed. This is what Gandhi calls *soul-force* which he often contrasts with brute-force.

While brute-force is based on egotism which creates conflict and misery, soul-force is based on love, trust, and humility which create harmony and happiness. Gandhi lays great emphasis on humility. *Genuine humility* is, however, very

5. *Ibid.*, pp. 9–10.

different from consciously affected modesty. It is a natural attitude which characterizes a man who has realized the insignificance and helplessness of the little self apart from God and humanity. It is to be found most in him who has surrendered his little self completely to the will of God and has made himself a mere instrument to it.

WORK BY SELF-SURRENDER

To be a mere instrument in the hands of God is to avoid all selfish motives. It is to try to do "the greatest good of all." It liberates man from the ever-increasing bondage of selfish desires which work with selfish motives always creates. It helps him also avoid the ordinary depression from failure and the madness from success, and helps him thereby to pursue steadily the path of duty with calm judgment. This ensures, on the one hand, the greatest success of the work done, and it brings, on the other hand, the most abiding peace and satisfaction to the worker.

This is the state of equability (*samabhava*) which is taught in the *Gita* and which Gandhi adopted as his ideal. So his motto was: "Work without attachment as a mere instrument to the will of God." This was also *true renunciation* for Gandhi. One should not fly from the world and one's duties. One should renounce the selfish desires for enjoying the fruits of action. The more one thinks of the pleasures to be attained, the less can one concentrate energy on the action. Do the will of God and let Him take care of the results. "Seek ye first the Kingdom of God and His righteousness; and all these things shall be added unto you." If the duties are rightly done, good results are sure to follow; for God's law rules the world.

But what does the will of God really mean? God is a name we give to the best motive forces of love, sympathy, and harmony that work in man, make for unity, and prevent chaos and ruin. Conscience or the sense of duty indicates the direction of these forces. It is, therefore, called the voice of God. To work for God is to follow conscience. To the extent that man can do so, he does only what is good for all and not merely for his little ego. The true good of the individual lies in the good of all which, of course, includes him too.

God is the name, again, of the abiding Reality that expresses itself through the changing phenomena of birth, decay, and death. To work for God is to work for this abiding principle. It gives strength to man to think that he is a link in the eternal principle of existence that survives death and destruction. Gandhi says: "We are living in the midst of death. What is the value of 'working for our own schemes' when they might be reduced to naught . . . ? *But we may feel strong as a rock, if we could truthfully say 'we work for God and His schemes.'* . . .Then nothing perishes." [6]

DYNAMIC HUMILITY AND PEACE

A life of service, dedicated to the best and the most abiding principles of existence, tends to efface the little self and it generates spontaneous and *dynamic humility*. For, the little self tends to be replaced by the Universal Self, the helpless

6. *YI*, September 23, 1926.

life by the Cosmic Life that moves all existence. Selfish desires then hide in shame. Selfless activity brings abiding joy,
and ceaseless service creates unceasing peace. So Gandhi says:

A life of service must be one of humility. . . . *True humility
means strenuous and constant endeavour* entirely directed towards the service of humanity. God is continuously in action
without resting for a single moment. If we would serve Him or
become one with Him, our activity must be as unwearied as His.
. . . *This restlessness constitutes true rest.* This never-ceasing
agitation holds the key to peace ineffable.[7]

This is what Gandhi said in defining the ideals of his home
of service, the Satyagraha Ashrama. His whole life of ceaseless service re-echoes this ideal and shows also the possibility
of the practice of it in private and public life.

Some Moral Maxims

We may mention here some moral maxims which Gandhi
accepted and found useful in life.

The greatest good of all.[8]—The ideal of service should be
pitched as high as possible. Our flesh is weak and it always
tends to slip back into lethargy and selfishness if there is the
slightest loophole. The motto of utilitarians, "the greatest
good of the *greatest* number," does not appeal to Gandhi.
The utilitarian derives his principle from the pleasure-seeking
motive present in every individual. "The utilitarian to be logical will never sacrifice himself." But one who bases his moral
principle, not on man's selfish search for pleasure, but on the
love and reason that are also present in him, sees his larger

7. *FYM*, pp. 47 f.; cf. *Gita*, Chap. III.
8. *YI*, December 9, 1926.

interest in the interest of all. His ideal should, therefore, be the greatest good of all. Gandhi's insistence on this principle also implies that in democratic rule by majority there is always the danger of neglecting the interest of the minority if we aim at only "the greatest number" and not "all." The simplest principle that we can remember for realizing this ideal is: *As with the self so with the universe.*

The goal ever recedes from us.—Though Gandhi was in favor of setting the ideal high he was always aware that the goal can never be completely reached. Unlike a follower of Shankara's Advaita Vedanta, but very like the Theistic Vedantins and most Western idealists, he repeatedly affirmed the unattainability of perfection in human life. As he explains:

> *No one can attain perfection while he is in the body* for the simple reason that the ideal state is impossible so long as one has not completely overcome his ego, and ego cannot be wholly gotten rid of so long as one is tied down by the shackles of the flesh. . . . The goal ever recedes from us. The greater the progress the greater the recognition of our unworthiness. *Satisfaction lies in the effort,* not in the attainment. *Full effort is full victory.*[9]

Man's duty is, therefore, to try for greater and greater progress though he can never reach absolute perfection.

The necessity for an unattainable ideal is to evoke greater and greater effort and to keep up the ceaseless spirit of further and further progress. As Tolstoy says, if we have to cross a swift stream we must have to aim our steering at a point much higher up the stream than where we wish to go. Changing the analogy Gandhi often says that perfect geometrical figures, like straight lines, can never be drawn, yet

9. *Ibid.,* September 20, 1928, and March 9, 1922.

because of these ideals we draw more and more perfect figures.

One step enough for me.[10]—In our ceaseless effort to reach the ideal we should not forget the present realities surrounding us and through which we have to reach the goal. "The future is unknown. We can take care only of the present which is in our hands. If we utilize the present well, then alone we can ensure future progress. We must take well the present step." This maxim reflects Gandhi's practical realism which existed side by side with his great idealism. He was fond of saying, "I am a practical idealist."

As the means so the end.—The present action of man determines his future—as the Indian law of Karma asserts. If the present action is immoral it will degrade the doer, spoil his habits, and he cannot therefore achieve a good and noble life. Our good habits are the most important capital of our lives, as William James used to say. The mere spectacular success which is sometimes attained by the adoption of foul means should not be mistaken for real success. No success is worthy of human effort if it does not ennoble man. If the man is lost, success becomes a pity and a shame. So says Gandhi: "They say 'means are after all means.' I would say 'means are after all everything.' As the means so the end. There is no wall of separation between means and end." [11] A bad means can never produce a really good end. It is very superficial to think, therefore, that a good end justifies a bad means. All means should be utilized to make man morally better and therefore the use of foul means is morally unjustifiable. As the Bible says: "For what shall it profit a man if he

10. BSG, p. 10.
11. *Ibid.*, p. 36.

shall gain the whole world, and lose his own soul?" This maxim was particularly adopted by Gandhi in avoiding all methods of political emancipation based on hatred and violence. He felt sure that such methods though temporarily successful would degrade the nation and involve it in a never-ending series of future bloodshed and ruin.

The true source of rights is duty.—We cannot morally acquire the right to expect any consideration from others, society, or state, unless we also do our duty towards them. "If we all discharge our duties, rights will not be far to seek. If leaving duties unperformed we run after rights, they will escape us like a will o' the wisp." [12]

Man and his deed are two distinct things.[13]—Gandhi followed this maxim, and commended it to his associates when he had to fight against the misdeeds of individuals or public organizations or systems. Believing in the inner goodness of men, Gandhi, like Christ, thought it wise to hate sins but not the sinner. He would, therefore, regard the misdeeds apart from miscreants whose good sense he would try to evoke by friendly appeal. A corollary to this maxim, which Gandhi used while fighting against the British Government in India, was: "Hate not the British but the British system." This attitude prevented much bitterness.

Heal thyself.—This is a very important maxim Gandhi adopted and found most useful in private and public life. He strongly believed that a man cannot really reform others unless he reformed himself. Example is much more effective than precept. Moreover, if a man follows the path of love in dealing with others and correcting their misbehavior he must

12. *YI*, January 8, 1925.
13. *Autobiography*, p. 337.

inspire respect, trust, and love; and this can be done only when he honestly tries to remove his own defects. Gandhi also realized that a man's or a nation's own faults and sins incite in others the baser passions like hatred, greed, plunder, and oppression.

In dealing with all such things Gandhi's first step was *self-analysis* and the second *self-purification*. This is the method he applied also in his political struggles. He analyzed and diagnosed, like Lord Buddha, the causes of India's suffering and found them to consist chiefly in communal differences, social injustice to backward classes, want of self-sufficiency particularly in clothes, want of proper education, and above all fear of the rulers. He applied himself heart and soul to the removal of these national defects by organizing constructive work in all these directions in all parts of the country. His political action thus proceeded side by side with the constructive efforts for national self-purification.[14]

The Cardinal Virtues

Though the different systems of Indian philosophy differed widely on metaphysical questions, there was a great unanimity among them in Ethics. All of them, except the Charvaka materialists, believed that the world was governed (either automatically or through God) by moral laws which ensured the conservation of values. "As you sow, so you will reap." No good work goes without good results and no bad work goes unpunished. This is the essence of the law of Karma which all the aforesaid Indian systems and religious schools accepted. Gandhi also adhered to this moral belief

14. *BSG*, pp. 124 f., and *YI*, April 6, 1921.

and found in it a great source of encouragement for a good moral life—for doing his duty for the sake of duty, unperturbed by any anxiety for the results of his actions. This moral attitude has an essential similarity to that of the great western philosopher Immanuel Kant who advocated the performance of duty for duty's sake without being moved by any thought of pleasurable consequences and with the faith that God sees that good deeds are ultimately followed by happiness.

There is a general unanimity among the Indian thinkers about the necessity of some cardinal virtues which *everyone* should try to practice, such as harmlessness (*ahimsa*), truthfulness (*satya*), nonstealing (*asteya*), chastity (*brahmacharya*) and nonacceptance, that is, nonpossession of unnecessary things (*aparigraha*). These five virtues are recognized by the Upanishads, the Buddhists, the Jainas, the Yoga system, and most others, though they are interpreted more or less rigorously by the different thinkers. Manu, the greatest of Indian law-givers, while laying down the universal duties for all (as distinguished from the special duties of the particular classes of society) mentions the first three of the five great virtues, and instead of the last two he mentions purity (physical and mental) and self-control (control of the senses, motor organs, and mind).

Gandhi accepted the former five traditional virtues and interpreted them in the light of his own experience and studies to suit the needs of the times and the conditions in which he and his co-workers lived, and the social and political work in which all were engaged. In fact he adds some more to the standard five for himself and the inmates of his Ashrama. Tolstoy's interpretation of the commandments of the Bible

influenced and strengthened Gandhi's interpretation of the
five vows to a great extent.

For the perfect practice of the cardinal virtues or any other
principle Gandhi accepted the general Indian formula "in
thought, in speech, and in action" (*manasa, vachasa, kayena*).
This is essentially also the teaching of the Bible. The subtle
beginning of an action, good or bad, is in the mind. Speech
is the next outer manifestation of it. It reaches consummation
in actual bodily activity. So Jesus thinks that he who lusts
in mind commits adultery. There is no wall dividing the
different levels of human life. Purity cannot be fully attained
until the entire life of thought, speech, and action becomes
pure. Moreover, if the subtle seed is not weeded out it will
take root and germinate in unperceived ways. Total purity—
the practice of virtue in thought, speech, and body—should,
therefore, be our goal, to leave no loophole for the devil.
This idea became all the more confirmed in Gandhi because
truth was for him the root of existence, and there could be
no room for hypocrisy which allows "one thing in mind, another in speech and something else in action." To strengthen
the will Gandhi preferred to take vows (*vratas*) to observe
the moral rules.

Let us now discuss briefly Gandhi's ideas about the five
traditional cardinal virtues and the ones he added to them
for the practice of which he and the inmates of his Ashrama
took solemn vows.

1. *Ahimsa: literally noninjury, and hence nonkilling.*—
It was used in this sense in the Upanishads, Buddhism, and
Jainism, and the orthodox Hindu laws of Manu. But it was
most rigorously interpreted by Jainism which set the ideal
of not killing or injuring any form of life for any purpose

at all, not even thinking or speaking of killing or injuring, and not even causing or permitting others to kill. They only relaxed the principle for the laity, allowing them to eat the nonmoving living organisms like plants. On the other hand, Manu, whom most Hindus followed, made the principle rather elastic, allowing the killing of animals for sacrifice and food and even the killing of men in self-defense. For him, though the ideal of desisting from killing is a very commendable one, it can be completely practised only by the few topmost persons in society. We have to make concessions for others.

But the position of Gandhi is midway between the two. As he says in the *Autobiography*, he does not accept Manu's concessions to the weakness of the flesh. Gandhi's attitude here, as elsewhere, is like that of Tolstoy. We must aim at the sky if we want to hit the top of a tree. The flesh is weak enough; to lay down rules of concession is to sanctify the failings of the flesh by sanction. So he stuck to the absolute ideal of *ahimsa*. He was closer to the Jainas than Manu, and he was much influenced by them since childhood. But in practice Gandhi could not satisfy the high and rigid standards of the Jainas. He could not allow pests and vermin to thrive at the cost of men. And when a mortally sick calf in his Ashrama was declared incurable by the doctor and was groaning in excruciating pain he permitted the doctor to put an end to its miserable life by some injection. So he brought down upon himself the wrath and rebuke of the pious Jainas and the orthodox Hindus. Gandhi, we saw, even helped the war efforts of the British on several occasions, and his action baffled the understanding of even some of his best friends and co-workers. What was really the justification, if any, of his behavior apparently contrary to his high and uncompromising ideals?

In his *Autobiography* he opens his mind and shows the dilemma that the true believer in perfect *ahimsa* is put into in practical life. "Man cannot for a moment live without consciously or unconsciously committing outward *himsa*. The very fact of living—eating, drinking, and moving about—necessarily involves some *himsa*, destruction of life, be it ever so minute." (p. 427)

If this be the fact, then why should we try to do the impossible and not be realistic? Gandhi was sufficiently realistic, but he was not prepared to stop with the *status quo* in the name of realism. That would really be half-realism. As a worshipper of complete Truth or Reality he could not ignore the reality of love in the human heart which has made human progress possible. "Non-violence is the law of our species." [15] To deaden this real and divine impulse in man by thoughtless cruelty is to hamper progress and pave the way to hell on earth. We must keep alive that divine spark and struggle as best possible to strengthen it by the practice of love and compassion. Struggling for the ideal is all that is given to man. "Full effort is full victory." Our goodness is to be judged, as Kant rightly pointed out, by the goodness of the will, "There is nothing unqualifiedly good, but the good will." For, success is controlled by circumstances, all of which are not within our control. So Gandhi continues in the passage referred to:

A votary of ahimsa therefore remains true to his faith if the spring of all his actions is compassion, if he shuns to the best of his ability the destruction of the tiniest creature, tries to save it,

15. *YI*, August 11, 1920.

and thus incessantly strives to be free from the deadly coil of himsa. He will be constantly growing in self-restraint and compassion, but he can never become entirely free from outward *himsa*. (*Autobiography*, pp. 427 f.)

The important points to note are, (1) that the main spring of *ahimsa* or nonviolence is love and the true criterion of nonviolence is, therefore, this inner feeling in the heart; (2) that if we do not ignore the inner call of love, we are obliged to desist from injury to living beings *as far as we can;* (3) that it is wrong to think, therefore, that since we cannot observe complete nonviolence, we should not try to observe the little we can; and (4) finally that the more we try to practice love and compassion the more can we increase them and can become morally elevated and truly happy.

It follows from the above that true nonviolence is not simply nonkilling, that is, outwardly desisting from injury; it must be from the bottom of one's heart; and therefore it must remove from the mind anger, hatred, and the spirit of revenge. One who harbors these evil feelings but only remains outwardly nonviolent out of fear does not at all observe real *ahimsa*. He is a hypocrite and a coward. Nonviolence or *ahimsa* is really for the strong and not for cowards and the weak. Gandhi says, therefore: "My creed of nonviolence is an extremely active force. It has *no room for cowardice or even weakness*." [16] He even goes so far as to hold, "I do believe that, where there is only a choice between cowardice and violence, I would advise violence."

With a psychological insight Gandhi sees that, in most cases, *violence is the expression of fear*. It is out of fear from known and unknown sources that man arms himself and goes

16. *Ibid.*, June 16, 1927.

out to attack others. One who has love enough for others does not entertain any fear from them.

However paradoxical it might sound, *violence is really the expression of an inner sense of weakness.* One who is strong in heart sheds fear with the help of love and is prepared even to sacrifice his body rather than harm others. He cannot be violent. His is ideal and real nonviolence. He can disarm the fear and suspicion of the enemy by his fearless love. He will melt the enemy's heart and arouse compassion in him by rather subjecting himself to suffering than harming the enemy. If he is strong enough in love and compassion he will even sacrifice, if necessary, his own life. Such a person paves the way for increasing peace all around. On the contrary, violence bred by fear and hatred breeds more of fear, hatred, and violence, and both the parties concerned are gripped by an increasing spate of these base and dreadful emotions. They bring ruin to themselves and others. Violence degrades both the parties, whereas nonviolence elevates them and ennobles both. As Buddha taught: "Enmity is never appeased by enmity; enmity is appeased by non-enmity. This is the eternal law." (Dhammapada, 1.5)

But in spite of all his enthusiasm for nonviolence Gandhi realized that in *some exceptional cases* killing may be necessary, for example, when a dog becomes rabid and there is no chance of recovery it should be killed. Again, "Suppose a man runs amuck and goes furiously about sword in hand, and killing any one that comes in his way, and no one dares to capture him alive. Anyone who despatches this lunatic, will earn the gratitude of the community and be regarded as a benevolent man." [17]

17. BSG, p. 156.

As the ultimate criterion of nonviolence is, for Gandhi, love and selflessness at heart, killing becomes a duty in some rare cases when these very noble sentiments require it. But these exceptional cases should not set the rule and encourage violence. The flesh is ready enough for allowing the devil to wreck the spirit and all that the spirit loves. The only question is how to keep the devil away by organizing and strengthening more and more the noble forces in us.[18]

From the above discussion it would be seen that though the word *ahimsa* originally conveyed the negative sense of noninjury, it was interpreted and used by Gandhi in the positive sense as well. Noninjury for him was a virtue in so far as it expressed love and good-will. So he sometimes translated *ahimsa* with the word love. By his life and teachings he put into his concept of *ahimsa* all that Buddha meant by friendliness (*maitri*) and compassion (*Karuna*), and also what Christ meant when he taught, "Love your enemies, bless them that curse you, do good to them that hate you." [19] *Ahimsa* carried, for Gandhi, also the positive spirit of treating all beings as one's very self (*atmavat sarvabhuteshu*) repeatedly taught in the *Gita* and other Indian scriptures. He thought that it was also the teaching of the Koran rightly interpreted. *Ahimsa* appeared, therefore, to him to be the very quintessence of the teachings of the great religions.

He finds confirmation of the idea of the supremacy of nonviolence in the current Sanskrit dictum, "*ahimsa* is the highest virtue" (*ahimsa paramo dharmah*). But why should it be regarded as the highest virtue? The reason is, he briefly writes in his diary (November 21, 1944), that without *ahimsa* Truth

18. *Ibid.*, pp. 154–62.
19. Matthew 5:44.

cannot be realized.[20] Truth for him was God that pervaded all beings, and preserved and unified them through love. God can be realized by loving God, and to love God is to love the beings in whom He is incarnate. So he says, "When you want to find Truth as God the only inevitable means is Love, i.e. non-violence." [21]

We may add that there are two other important reasons as to why *ahimsa* should be regarded as the supreme virtue. The first reason is that *ahimsa* as noninjury to life is the logical presupposition of all other duties towards living beings, since we cannot do *any* duty towards a fellow being unless he is alive. The second reason is that *ahimsa* as love is the parent of all the other cardinal virtues.

2. *Satya: truthfulness.*—This is the next cardinal virtue on which Gandhi lays the utmost emphasis. The Sanskrit word *satya* means not only truth, but also truthfulness, as the word "truth" also sometimes does in English. The possibility of this change in meaning shows that there is an intrinsic connection between truth and truthfulness. Regard for truth generates the truthfulness in thought, speech, and action.

Truthfulness in the sphere of thought means, for Gandhi, devotion to facts and eagerness to discover the truth of any matter before arriving at any decision. We have seen how he practised this principle in private and public life, and how he made his whole life a series of experiments for the discovery of diverse kinds of truths. Like all ancient Indian philosophers he held, "Ignorance is at the root of failures." [22] Careful observation, sifting of evidence, and the dispassion-

20. *Bapu ke ashirvad*, p. 5.
21. *YI*, December 31, 1931.
22. *H*, April 24, 1937.

ate use of reason were the methods which he used for the discovery of truth. In any conflict between reason and authority, whether personal or scriptural, however high, Gandhi would always follow reason. "I do not advocate," says he, "surrender of God-given reasoning faculty in the face of tradition." [23] Reason was the voice of God within him and whenever he felt puzzled he would retire into himself and try to clear the mind of the disturbing forces of passions and prejudices to be able to listen to the clear voice of reason which, he believed, allowed truth to shine out when the obstacles were removed. So he says, "Truth is by nature self-evident. As soon as you remove the cobwebs of ignorance that surround it, it shines clear." [24]

The discovery of truth requires, therefore, also self-analysis and self-purification. One cannot see the truth so long as he is under the influence of what Gandhi, following the tradition of Indian ethics, calls: "The six deadly enemies," namely, "lust, anger, greed, infatuation, pride and falsehood." [25] One who is morally strong can alone see the truth, and particularly so in controversial matters, and more particularly in practical social and political controversies.

What enabled Gandhi to stick to truthfulness in thought was his moral purity, his constant effort to keep away "the deadly enemies" and not to allow them to blind his vision and judgment. He could thus see the basic issues and truths more clearly than most of the statesmen with whom he had to deal, and whose minds were clouded by anxieties for vested interests. He could also feel and confess his own

23. *YI*, September 22, 1927.
24. *Ibid.*, May 27, 1926.
25. *H*, September 15, 1940.

errors and failings without feeling embarrassed by any false sense of political or social prestige. In one of his early political campaigns of nonviolence against the British Government in India, when he found that it led to violent outbursts in some places, he called off the movement and declared that it was a great "Himalayan blunder" on his part "to have called upon the people to launch upon civil disobedience before they had qualified themselves for it." For the time being this exposed him to the ridicule of the Government and the bitter resentment of many of his followers. But the confession of the mistake made him internally stronger, purer, and more cautious in the subsequent political movements by which gradually he broke the many fetters of foreign rule in India. His unflinching honesty and sincerity won the hearts of the followers as well as of many of his opponents and ultimately made him the strongest leader of moral fights.

Truthfulness in speech and action is the natural outcome of the truthfulness in thought. Gandhi was internally convinced of the truth of the ancient Indian dictum "Truth alone prevails" (*Satyam eva jayate*)—which, incidentally, has now been adopted by the independent republic of India as its official motto. This conviction made him always think that the deceiver must be ultimately deceived. He would also sometimes try to prove logically the superiority of truth and the hollowness of falsehood by the following clever and witty argument: Even when falsehood momentarily succeeds, it does so by passing under the garb of truth. So the strength of falsehood is ultimately derived from its simulating truth. Truth alone has thus the intrinsic power that can make it prevail. Falsehood has no legs of its own to stand upon. It is doomed by its own nature to ultimate destruction.

Truthfulness in speech and action flows spontaneously from the love of fellow beings. Loving a person genuinely and deceiving him by words or action are incompatible attitudes. Truth and love are therefore inseparable in Gandhi's thought.

From love also follows the ideal vow of truthfulness as conceived by the Indian moralists and as followed by Gandhi. This vow is *to speak what is true and good and pleasant*. To speak what is simply true may descend to frivolity, garrulity, obscenity, and the like and it would benefit neither the speaker nor the person spoken to. Love for the latter would require the speaker to speak only what would be good or beneficial (*hita* or *pathya*) to him. Again speaking even a beneficial truth in a harsh or rude manner could do more harm than good by causing repulsion and resistance. It would be inconsistent with love. Truth should therefore be spoken also in a pleasant (*priyam*) way. Truth-speaking thus becomes an art which can be perfected only by constant effort in every sphere of life. This is the vow that Gandhi took and tried to realize in speech and in writing. Referring to the Sanskrit text that lays down the ideal of truth-speaking, he comments: "In my opinion the Sanskrit text means that one should speak the truth in gentle language. One had better not speak it, if one cannot do so in a gentle way; meaning thereby that there is not truth in a man who cannot control his tongue." [26]

This ideal and the deep conviction about the basic superiority of truthfulness were reflected in Gandhi's entire life—

26. *YI*, September 17, 1925. The text is: "Satyam bruyat, priyam bruyat, na bruyat satyam apriyam."—Manu 4.138; also in other works.

his talks, speeches, writings, and dealings, in all of which he avoided exaggeration, intolerance, harshness, and anxiety for scoring cheap victory. So, as a conversationalist, as a public speaker and debater, as a mouthpiece of the dumb millions, as a journalist, and as a leader of the severest political struggles, he set a model of gentle and effective truthfulness scarcely to be found before in recorded history.

3. *Asteya: nonstealing.*—The observance of this virtue consists in not taking away the property of anyone else unless it is given by the latter. It is based, therefore, on the recognition of the right of everyone to his own property. The Jaina thinkers point out that property is "the outer life of a person," and to rob him of property is to rob him of his life.[27] In other words, the life of a person is impossible without some possession and if we recognize it as a duty not to injure his life, we must not rob him of his possession. This virtue also follows from love. To love a person and to deprive him of his property are not compatible attitudes. Stealing is bad, thinks Gandhi, because it injures others. So the meaning of nonstealing as a vow is for him not simply desisting from committing what is ordinarily known as theft, but also desisting from all kinds of exploitation at the cost of others, such as the capitalist's appropriation of the fruits of the labor of the workers. In all such exploitation he saw the presence of harm to life (*himsa*).

Gandhi goes even a step further in his interpretation of the vow of nonstealing by holding that "taking or keeping of things which we do not require is also a kind of stealing" which must, therefore, be shunned. This rigorous interpretation which we find in his diary (November 24, 1944) makes

27. See *Sarva-darshana-Sangraha*, Jaina system.

this vow almost indistinguishable from the traditional vow of *aparigraha.*

4. *Aparigraha: literally nonacceptance.*—It was interpreted and practised more or less rigorously by different schools. Extreme nonacceptance would mean giving up all ownership. It was known as the vow of not possessing anything (*akinchan-vrata*). This was meant only for the hermits who would completely depend on nature's wild fruits, roots, and cereals, or on unsolicited gifts from men. But, for the ordinary persons of society this was an impossibly high ideal. So it came to mean nonacceptance of any unnecessary thing. Necessity being an elastic thing, this vow again admitted of different degrees of severity.

Gandhi's ideal in respect of this vow was "not to accumulate things not necessary for the day," as he put it in his diary of November 25, 1944.

It must be borne in mind that such an ideal he put before himself and his selfless band of social and national workers. He wanted all of them to have faith in God and to prepare themselves for the service of God in men by self-surrender. They should be prepared to sacrifice even their bodies, not to speak of other possessions and desires for accumulation of wealth. So he says:

"Possession implies provision for the future. . . . God never stores for the morrow. . . . If, therefore, we repose faith in His providence, we should rest assured that He will give us every day our daily bread, meaning everything that we require." [28]

His faith in God served Gandhi very well. His work and his workers never suffered for want of money. Whenever

28. *FYM*, p. 23.

he was in financial difficulty help came in from unexpected and often unknown sources; and his faith became more and more strengthened.

He realized that "Love and exclusive possession can never go together." Perfect love would demand readiness to give up everything including the body. But that is an ideal towards which we should move, though we can never realize it completely in life. He writes, therefore:

Theoretically when there is perfect love, there must be perfect non-possession. The body is our last possession. So a man can only exercise perfect love and be completely dispossessed, if he is prepared to embrace death and renounces his body for the sake of human service.

But that is true in theory only. In actual life, we can hardly exercise perfect love, for the body as a possession, will always remain with us. Man will ever remain imperfect, and it will always be his part to try to be perfect. So that perfection in love or non-possession will remain an unattainable ideal as long as we are alive, but towards which we must ceaselessly strive.[29]

5. *Brahmacharya: continence.*—This has also been differently interpreted and practised as a cardinal virtue. Etymologically it means the way of life dedicated to, or practise of, Brahma. Brahma means both God and the Vedas. But the general meaning of the word (*brahmacharya*) is a life of celibacy which was regarded essential both for a student of the Vedas and also for one who would devote himself exclusively to the realization of God. Along with celibacy were associated all kinds of self-restraint. Manu considers absolute desisting from sexual relation as essential for the first quarter of a man's life as a student. But during the second quarter of his life every healthy, able-bodied man should marry and raise a family. Even then he should

29. *BMR*, p. 412.

exercise sex-control by loyalty to the married consort and by observing some other restrictions. Even the life of such chastity and self-control was regarded by Manu as good as celibacy. For a person after fifty, particularly for one of the intellectual class, absolute sex-control is again considered desirable by Manu.

Gandhi's conception of *brahmacharya* was based on these ancient ideas modified by his own experience and needs. He wanted to devote his entire energy to social and political work. He found self-continence invaluable for this purpose. Moreover, if a social worker had growing family responsibilities his work would suffer. He, therefore, set for himself and his co-workers the ideals of absolute continence. So the unmarried workers tried to observe this ideal by remaining single and the married by restraining themselves. Celibacy and continence thus came to be recognized as the essential requisite of the life of a selfless social worker.

It was, however, the most difficult ideal that Gandhi tried to achieve by a life-long struggle through failure and increased determination. In all these struggles he realized that the capacity for sex-control is dependent upon general self-control, the general power of inhibition. It can be increased, therefore, only by increasing self-control in every sphere of life, in thought, in speech and in action. Love of the flesh, he further realized, could be effectively overcome by replacing it by the higher love and attraction for God. So he developed the following conception of *brahmacharya:*

Its root meaning may be given thus: that conduct which puts one in touch with God.

The conduct consists in the fullest control over all the senses. . . .

Popularly it has come to mean mere physical control over the

organ of generation. This narrow meaning has debased brahmacharya and made its practice all but impossible. Control over
the organ of generation is impossible without proper control
over all the senses. They are all interdependent. Mind on the
lower plane is included in the senses. Without control over the
mind mere physical control,even if it can be attained for a time,
is of little or no use.

The mind is even more difficult to curb than the wind. Never-
theless the existence of God within makes even the control of
the mind possible. Let no one think that it is impossible because
it is difficult.[30]

Among other kinds of control necessary for the control
of the sexual appetite Gandhi considered "the control of the
palate" the most important. This is one of the chief reasons
that led him to carry on life-long experiments on diet to
observe the effect of food on sex-impulse. The effect of
food on mind is an ancient Indian belief which Gandhi tried
to verify in his life with the help of some modern ideas about
the basic constituents of food necessary for human life.

Though Gandhi observed such strict rules regarding eating, drinking, and other matters, what appeared to others
as great rigor became to him quite easy and natural. So he
did not feel and think that he was practising any ascetic
mortification of the flesh, as he writes, "It is wrong to call
me an ascetic. The ideals that regulate my life are presented
for acceptance by mankind in general." [31]

6. *Abhaya: fearlessness.*—To the five cardinal virtues
Gandhi added another, namely, *abhaya* (fearlessness) which
also is mentioned sometimes in the ancient scriptures, like

30. *BSG*, pp. 248 f.
31. *Ibid.*, p. 248.

the Upanishads. This was specially important as a vow for
workers who were trained to face death and untold suffering
in their nonviolent fight against powers armed with deadly
weapons. He derived it also from love and regarded it necessary for spiritual life. He explains the idea of fearlessness in
his diary (November 26, 1944) thus: "Fearlessness implies
absence of all kinds of fears. It is the freedom from such fears
as the fear of death, molestation, hunger, humiliation, criti-
cism and wrath of others, and fear of ghosts, spirits, etc."

As to the necessity of it he says: "Cowards can never be
moral." . . . "Fearlessness is indispensable for the growth
of the other noble qualities. How can one seek Truth, or
cherish Love, without fearlessness?" [32]

Moral bravery is for Gandhi the highest heroism. And it
consists not in striking and injuring others but in the readiness to sacrifice, patiently and fearlessly, everything including life for the good of other fellow beings, out of love for
them.

The attainment of the cardinal virtues through a life of
intense activity in every sphere of duty was the firm vow of
Gandhi and the members of his Ashrama. In the rigid interpretation of these vows he also got a good deal of inspiration from the five commandments of the Sermon on the
Mount particularly as they were interpreted by Tolstoy in
the fourth chapter of his *The Kingdom of God Is Within
You*. Gandhi's conceptions of nonviolence and nonpossession seem to have been specially influenced by Tolstoy's
ideas.

In addition to the six virtues mentioned above, Gandhi

32. *Ibid.*, p. 243, and *FYM*, p. 27.

also recommended a few others as particularly necessary for modern India, such as bread labor, equal regard for all religions, removal of social inequality, and economic self-sufficiency.

Behind all these vows and virtues of Gandhi lay his simple spiritual perception of every being as the manifestation of the Self or God that is present in all. Love for all beings flowed from this perception and all virtues from this love. Gandhi was aware that love without the guidance of reason could degenerate into a blind passion. So he attached the greatest importance to reason as much for the knowledge of truth as for knowing what is right to do. Like Buddha he believed that constant vigilance and effort were necessary for a good moral life.

SOCIETY

As early as the *Rig Veda* we find the conception of the universe as an organic whole, and society is also conceived as an organism composed of different limbs. This idea is very clearly revealed by the hymn to Man (*Purusha-sukta*) in which the different classes of society are metaphorically described as forming the mouth, the arms, the thighs, and the feet of the Supreme Person who manifests Himself in the world and also remains mostly unmanifested. The different classes in Vedic society seem to have been based on the different necessary functions performed by individuals in accordance with their diverse natural aptitudes. They had not yet been stratified into rigid, unalterable, and hereditary castes which developed later in India. They were the natural classes to be found everywhere in the world.

THE NATURAL CLASSES

Gandhi accepted this original Indian conception of natural classes (*varnas*); but he severely criticized and tried to reform the later conception of castes which he regarded as an undesirable excrescence of the original ideal. The effective maintenance of the social organism, like that of the living body, requires division of labor as well as harmonious co-ordination. All kinds of labor—intellectual, military, commercial, agricultural, and merely manual—are necessary for society. They should, therefore, be performed in the spirit of duty. There should not arise, therefore, any discrimination against any kind of honest labor. All being equally valuable for society, all should carry equal wages. No class should consider itself higher and look down upon any other class. The question of special privileges or rights cannot arise if every kind of work enjoys equal dignity and is done with a sense of duty. Gandhi believes that the original ideal behind the much abused caste-system was based upon such a conception of natural classes (*varnas*). So he says:

I believe that every man is born in the world with certain natural tendencies. Every person is born with certain definite limitations which he cannot overcome. From a careful observation of those limitations the law of *varna* was deduced. It establishes certain spheres of action for certain people with certain tendencies. This avoided all unworthy competition. Whilst recognizing limitations the law of *varna* admitted no distinctions of high and low; on the one hand it guaranteed to each the fruits of his labours and on the other it prevented him from pressing upon his neighbour. This great law has been degraded and fallen into disrepute. But my conviction is that an ideal social order will only be evolved when the implications of this law are fully understood and given effect to.[33]

33. *BMR*, p. 413.

The fourfold Hindu classification of society originally embodied this principle. "The four divisions define duties, they confer no privileges. All are born to serve God's creation, a *brahmana* with knowledge, a *kshatriya* with his power of protection, a *vaishya* with his commercial ability and a *shudra* with his bodily labour." [34]

This does not mean that a man devoted to knowledge should neglect self-defense or hate bodily labor, and so on. It only means that the main occupation should be what a person has the greatest natural aptitude for. The organization of society on the basic principle of dutiful service and aptitude would encourage "self-restraint and conservation and economy of energy."

"The present caste-system," Gandhi recognized, "is the very antithesis of Varnashrama. The sooner public opinion abolishes it the better." . . . "Caste has nothing to do with religion. It is harmful both to spiritual and national growth." [35]

DIGNITY OF LABOR [36]

Though Gandhi was a lover of the ancient Indian ideal of the division of labor in accordance with natural aptitudes, he was aware from his experience of the lazy intellectuals, middle men, and aristocrats of India and other places, that if manual work were relegated to particular classes, both the work and the workers acquired a kind of social stigma. Without some amount of physical exertion the body also

34. *BSG*, p. 266.
35. *Ibid.*, p. 265.
36. See *ibid.*, pp. 46–62, for Gandhi's ideas on this entire topic of labor.

cannot be kept fit. Instead of spending time in one-sided intellectual work or luxury and then taking artificial exercises and medicines for keeping the body fit, everyone should do some amount of natural physical work daily needed for the maintenance of himself and his family. Ideal labor is tilling the ground in the open air for raising one's food. But as that is not possible for everyone, one can "spin or weave, or take up carpentry or smithery." "Everyone must be his own scavenger." Rough work should not be the exclusive work of any class. If everyone lends a hand to such work he will keep himself fit, appreciate and promote the dignity of labor and "the equality of man."

The necessity of "bread labour" was impressed on Gandhi's mind by Ruskin's book, *Unto this last*, and by Tolstoy's writings which publicized "The theory of bread labour first propounded in his country by the Russian peasant Bondaref." But Gandhi also found support for this theory in the Bible which says, "In the sweat of thy brow shalt thou eat thy bread." He finds further confirmation in the teaching of the *Gita* that he who eats without laboring for his food "eats stolen food." Enjoyment of any benefit without earning a right to it by some kind of labor appeared to Gandhi as a kind of stealing and an offense against the moral principle of nonstealing previously discussed.

ECONOMIC EQUALITY

As Gandhi believed that all kinds of work necessary for society are equally sacred duties for persons who possessed the special aptitudes for them, he held that there should be equal wages for all.

He believed in the division of labour or work. But he did insist on the equality of wages. *The lawyer, the doctor or the teacher was entitled to no more than the Bhangi (i.e. scavenger).* Then only would division of work uplift the nation or the earth. There was no other royal road to true civilization or happiness.[37]

He realized that it was too high an ideal to be attained at once. But still he thought that every country should set that goal and incessantly strive to attain it. Only then economic equilibrium, peace, and happiness could be attained, more and more. As soon as the ideal of equality of wages is accepted there will be a natural tendency on the part of every person to choose the kind of work which he likes most and can do best.

CAPITAL AND LABOR

Gandhi thought "that labour was far superior to capital. Without labour gold, silver and copper were a useless burden. It was labour which extracted precious ore from the bowels of the earth." [38] He thus came quite close to Marx's labor theory of value. He also thought like Marx that the combination of labor against capital could subvert capitalism. Yet he would not incite labor against capital, nor encourage the overthrow of capitalists *by force*. This latter process would be based on class hatred and undermine the moral principle of *ahimsa* (nonviolence or love). No society can thrive on hatred and violence in any form. Just as it is immoral for the capitalists to steal the legitimate fruits of the workers' labor, it is equally immoral for laborers to wreck the industries and tyrannize over the capitalists by exag-

37. *H*, March 23, 1947.
38. *Ibid.*, September 7, 1947.

gerated demands. Gandhi "wanted marriage between capital and labour." He wanted harmonious cooperation between the two. His whole moral philosophy and the belief in the inner goodness of man discounted the Marxist conception that class struggle was the basic truth of human history and that it must be accentuated more and more until the working class become the rulers of society and state.

THE TRUSTEESHIP OF THE RICH

On the contrary, he believed it possible, by appeal to the basic human principles of reason and love, to persuade capitalists to realize that the capital in their hands represented the fruit of the labor of the people and it should be treated as such. A capitalist, a landlord, or anyone else who happens to have now surplus wealth, should act as the *trustee* of the people's wealth and should spend it for the welfare of the people. He should realize now the evils and dangers of accumulation of wealth and also should see that it is to his own larger interest to use his wealth for the people, rather than for his personal comforts. "*Capitalists would then exist only as trustees*. When that happy day dawned, there would be no difference between capital and labour. Then labour will have ample food, good and sanitary dwellings, all the necessary education for their children, ample leisure for self-education and proper medical assistance." [39]

Gandhi obtained the idea of trusteeship from his legal studies in early life while he was in England. He found it also in the *Gita*. He tried to apply it to the solution of existing economic inequalities. He believed that inequalities could

39. *Ibid.*

not be rooted out of society unless all parties concerned, the poor and the rich, were morally awakened to the consciousness of their own duties, defects, and weaknesses. It is only an appeal to reason and love that can bring about such awareness and the consequent efforts for self-purification. To organize the poor by the cheap and ready appeal to their selfish instincts, their anger, arrogance, jealousy, and greed is to demoralize them in another way. Even if the laborers win, in violent fights, more money and physical comforts, they would be no nearer to real happiness. The defeated capitalists and their allies in other regions will invent all kinds of hindrances to prevent the spread of such a movement. Reformation by moral appeal and "change of heart" gradually gathers greater force and spreads by the power of its noble example to all parts of the world. Change by violent means sows the seed of contention, bitterness, and future destruction. The demoralized laborers who have not been taught to restrain their passions, but have only been combined by their common enmity to the capitalists, will violently disagree among themselves when they come into power, and destroy one another out of personal ambition. In fact the laborers will then behave like the unreasonable capitalists. A better way is to educate the laborers and the capitalists, and make them feel their moral responsibilities and the benefits of harmonious adjustment. The laborers can withdraw their cooperation and thereby paralyze the organizations and bring the capitalists to their senses regarding the necessity of harmonious cooperation.

But such action should be based on truth and nonviolence; that is to say, it must be based on true grievances and it should be carried out without inner enmity and hatred. Such a method is called by Gandhi *satyagraha*. It will be explained more fully later.

THE IDEAL ECONOMIC ORGANIZATION OF SOCIETY [40]

Though Gandhi's ideal was equality he recognized that there were some inherent limitations in the capacities of the individuals that could not be removed. Consequently if equal opportunities are given to the individuals, some would earn more than others even if the rates of wages be more or less equal for equal amount of work. To enforce absolute equality artificially by law would be to create a rigid steel frame which would have little initiative for individual enterprise and voluntary moral growth. This last can be achieved only by the creation of moral enthusiasm for following the basic moral principles of love or nonviolence, nonstealing and nonpossession. A nonviolent organization will prevent all kinds of exploitation. The principle of nonstealing would demand the recognition that everyone has a right to his own property and this right should not be violated. This would be a curb on the greed for the property of others and for anything not earned by one's own labor. On the other hand the principle of nonpossession would teach that everyone should limit his own possession to what is needed by him and spend the rest for the welfare of others. Though this is a difficult ideal, it is only by the promotion and encouragement of such moral attitudes and habits that society can really progress towards greater equality. Gandhi practically sums up the whole situation in the simple utterance, "If we have no love for our neighbour, no change, however revolu-

40. See *BSG*, Chaps. V and VI.

tionary, can do us good." [41] Maldistribution of wealth can never be effectively checked without the cultivation of the virtues that follow from the law of love.

THE MENACE OF INDUSTRIALISM [42]

The growth of industrialism appeared to Gandhi, as to Ruskin, as a menace to the basic moral ideals of human society. He saw in it an endless tangle of moral evils which can only be briefly mentioned here. The concrete background of his ideas was the conditions created in his own country by foreign industrialism. Industrialism depends on the procurement of vast quantities of raw material and a vast market for the sale of the finished goods. For both purposes the resources and the markets of foreign countries become necessary. Exploitation of the undeveloped countries becomes inevitable. Colonial expansion, imperialism, commercial monopoly, repeated war with other rival industrialized countries, diplomatic mechanisms for keeping down the economic and political growth of the rivals as well as of the exploited nations, the propagation of the myths of cultural, racial, and religious superiorities of the exploiters—all follow in a ceaseless train, demoralizing the whole world.

Moreover, the growth of large-scale industries based on the investment of large capital and the employment of large numbers of laborers breeds the equally large problems of the relation between capital and labor. Gandhi saw with disgust and horror the openly violent rebellions of laborers in Russia and other countries against the subtle violence

41. *YI*, October 7, 1926.
42. *BSG*, Chap. V.

of the capitalistic industrialists. He saw the same story repeated in India in the few industrial areas. He did not, therefore, think it wise for his country to try to establish and increase industrialism and invite all the troubles that had already beset the industrialized countries. An ancient Indian proverb contained the advice: Rather than handle mud and then wash your hands, do not touch mud at all.

Gandhi found that the growth of big industries in some Indian cities attracted the villagers to the crowded cities. The village homes were being broken, the healthy social ties and neighborly feelings were mostly gone. Individuals were lost in crowds where each person counted for a floating unit in huge and rushing systems the beginnings, ends, and purposes of which were very dimly realized by him. Man was reduced to a mere tool, a mere number. He lost his personality and his spontaneous moral sense, and scarcely felt the joy of creation enjoyed by the producer of a village handicraft. Life became a mechanical drudgery. Escape was sought in gross sensuous pleasures like drinking, gambling, and all the vices that follow from them. The whole process of industrial growth appeared to Gandhi as a monstrous process of mechanization, dehumanization, and demoralization, by which course individuals could never develop and realize the best in them.

Moreover Gandhi found that unlike in some countries where there was dearth of laborers, and machines were necessary for saving human labor, India had enough of laborers; the only question was how to employ them. The introduction of labor-saving machines in India would create more unemployment by throwing out of work persons who were engaged in manual work, cottage industries, and agriculture in the villages. The unemployed laborers could only be utilized by starting other industries to manufacture other kinds of goods and so on. The effect would be to multiply the evils of industrialization. Besides, the newly developing industries would mostly be devoted to the production of luxury goods creating more and more the insatiable demand for creature comforts. Human energy would be increasingly exhausted in search of pleasure. The motto would then become, "High living and plain thinking." The welfare of humanity lies in "Plain living and high thinking," not in the multiplication of material wants, but in curtailing the dispensable desires and in devoting maximum energy to the pursuit of spiritual values.

The Proper Use of Machines

It should not be supposed that Gandhi was opposed to machines. He was conscious that even the spinning wheel he tried to introduce into every Indian home was a machine, and he always encouraged research for its improvement. "Machinery has its place; it has come to stay. But it must not be allowed to displace necessary human labour." [43] What Gandhi objected to were (1) the introduction of machines which would create more unemployment, (2) exploitation of the poor laborers by the rich capitalists, and exploitation of one country by another, (3) the moral evils attending the mad craze for large-scale industries, centralization, and monopolies, and (4) man's limbs being atrophied by too much dependence on machines. So Gandhi says more clearly:

43. *YI*, November 5, 1925.

What I object to is the *craze* for machinery, not machinery as such. . . . Men go on "saving labour," till thousands are without work and thrown on the open streets to die of starvation. I want to save time and labour, not for a fraction of mankind, but for all; I want the concentration of wealth, not in the hands of few, but in the hands of all. Today machinery merely helps a few to ride on the back of millions. The impetus behind it all is not the philanthropy to save labour, *but greed.* It is against this constitution of things that I am fighting with all my might. . . . I am aiming, not at eradication of all machinery, but limitation. . . . *The supreme consideration is man.*[44]

Gandhi visualized for free India the limited manufacture of machines in nationalized or state-controlled factories.[45]

DECENTRALIZATION

Gandhi's life-long dream and effort were to develop self-contained villages based primarily on agriculture and cottage industry, aided if possible with simple and cheap machines. Decentralized and autonomous village communities in natural, healthy surroundings would help individuals live simpler lives, develop more of social sense, cooperative works, intimate neighborly love, and the virtues that follow therefrom. Defense would be much easier too. So Gandhi says, "I suggest that, if India is to evolve along non-violent lines, it will have to decentralize many things. Centralization cannot be sustained and defended without adequate force. Simple homes from which there is nothing to take away require no policing. . . ."[46] The repeated attacks on big cities and

44. *BSG*, p. 66.
45. *Ibid.*, p. 67.
46. *H*, December 30, 1939.

factory areas during the last two great wars strengthened this conviction in Gandhi's mind. "Centralization as a system is inconsistent with non-violent structure of society." But at the same time Gandhi did not want to develop exclusive villages, altogether cut off from the world. We shall discuss later Gandhi's conception of an ideal village republic.

EDUCATION

Gandhi realized the necessity of educational reconstruction for the general and political regeneration of his country. He and his followers devoted themselves to educational work in different parts of India. What is now known there as "the basic system of education" and is being tried extensively in the state of Bihar and other places, draws its inspiration from Gandhi's ideas of education. We should bear in mind that Gandhi worked as a teacher in his Ashramas and taught young children to read and write, and also to spin, to make sandals and other things. His ideas were primarily born of practical experience.

Following the etymological sense of education Gandhi says, "By education I mean an all-round drawing out of the best in the child and man—body, mind and spirit." [47] Every individual is born with certain capacities which can be developed to the best advantage of the individual and society by proper education. All-round development is possible only if education can combine knowledge with work, precept with example. The first responsibility lies with the parents whose action, thought, and feeling, according to Gandhi, in-

47. *Ibid.*, July 31, 1937.

fluence the child imperceptibly, but very deeply, even from the very time of conception. Unless the parents live up to high ideals, children cannot be properly trained.

Gandhi was a firm believer in the ancient Indian ideal of a student who was required to observe strict celibacy, to learn sense-control, and study for the first twenty-five years of his life. Celibacy and self-discipline are necessary for study; and they prepare the youth best for the world.

The early education of the child can be best imparted by word of mouth. A child can be taught ten times more by this method than through books, and much earlier than he can read and write.

Like John Dewey, Gandhi lays very great emphasis on "learning by doing." He says, "I hold that true education of the intellect can only come through a proper exercise and training of the bodily organs, e.g., hands, feet, eyes, ears, nose, etc. In other words an intelligent use of the bodily organs in a child provides the best and quickest way of developing his intellect." [48]

This lays down the philosophy of the basic education. According to this, a student is taught to use his organs of knowledge and action harmoniously in learning some basic crafts like carding cotton, spinning, weaving, carpentry, gardening, etc. All literary and scientific education centers round these crafts, supplying their intellectual background as well as the solution of problems arising out of such work.

By intelligent planning of courses covering all branches of knowledge and integrating them with manual work the students would be made physically efficient, intellectually alert, practically useful, and possessed of self-confidence. By

48. *Ibid.*, May 8, 1937.

following such a method the manual work done by the student would fetch some income which could meet at least a part of the cost of the school. The cost of education incurred by the state would thus be less, and spread of education would be facilitated. From his personal experience Gandhi says:

"I hold that the highest development of the mind and the soul is possible under such a system of education. Only every handicraft has to be taught not merely mechanically as it is done today but scientifically, i.e., the child should know the why and wherefore of every process." [49] Gandhi conceived this method primarily for the villages, so that the children of the communities could be trained up to follow one of the useful crafts there more scientifically. They would thus rehabilitate the villages and stem the tide of migration of the villagers towards cities. So he says: "You have to train the boys in one occupation or another. Round this special occupation you will train up his mind, his body, his handwriting, his artistic sense, and so on. He will be master of the craft he learns." [50]

He planned this system of education "as the spearhead of a *silent social revolution* fraught with most far-reaching consequences." The establishment of scientific and efficient cottage industries would eliminate the evils of industrialization. "And all this would be accomplished without the horror of a bloody class-war or a colossal capital expenditure such as would be involved in the mechanization of a vast continent like India. Nor would it entail a helpless dependence on foreign imported machinery or technical skill." [51]

49. *Ibid.*, July 31, 1937.
50. *Ibid.*, September 18, 1937.
51. *Ibid.*, October 9, 1937.

The basic system of education is still in an experimental state in India. Gandhi's dreams of making the villages self-supporting on the basis of agriculture and some basic crafts yet remain mostly unrealized. Some plans for harmonious adjustment between large-scale industries and efficient cottage industries are, however, now under way. The tide of industrialism is sweeping over every land since the last war. Gandhi's ideas have not yet received a fair trial, neither perhaps would they do so until the present system is confronted by some crises that can turn the tide.

Gandhi was strongly in favor of teaching art, music, and drill to develop the aesthetic and rhythmic sense of the young people. All true art is "the expression of the soul." "Music means rhythm, order. Its effect is electrical. It immediately soothes." "There is a rhythm and music in drill that makes action effortless and eliminates fatigue." All these should be combined to ensure the all-round development of the young.[52]

Gandhi was not in favor of so-called higher education which consisted in mere intellectual training unrelated to the real needs of the society and the individual. So he wrote, "I would revolutionize college education and relate it to national necessities."[53] But he added, "Thus I claim that I am not an enemy of higher education. . . . Under my scheme there will be more and better libraries, more and better laboratories, more and better research institutes. . . . The knowledge gained by them will be the common property of the people."[54]

Character building, the development of strength, cour-

52. *BSG*, pp. 303–6.
53. *H*, July 31, 1937.
54. *BSG*, p. 297.

age, virtue, the ability to forget oneself in working towards great aims, this was for Gandhi the goal of education. Literacy or academic learning was "only a means to this great end."[55] But character would not be built by mere instruction. Moral education could be possible by the influence of the good character of the parents and teachers who must, therefore, strive "to take care of their p's and q's" in every minute act of daily life.

Gandhi did not support the idea of imparting denominational religious instruction in state institutions, as it would lead to all kinds of complication. "This did not mean that the state schools would not give ethical teaching. The fundamental ethics were common to all religions." [56]

Gandhi believed in national education which would promote a love for the best things in one's own national culture and confidence in one's own national potentialities. Without these no individual or nation could rise. But at the same time the aim of education should be to help the individual and the nation to develop their potential capacities along their own lines towards the realization of human unity and international amity. "No culture can live, if it attempts to be exclusive." He writes in *Young India* (June 1, 1921), "I do not want my house to be walled in on all sides and my windows to be stuffed. I want the cultures of all lands to be blown about my house as freely as possible. But I refuse to be blown off my feet." If the individual or the nation has no leg of its own to stand upon it cannot possibly help or embrace others.

Like all the great modern Indian thinkers, Gandhi was a

55. *Ibid.*, p. 287.
56. *H*, March 16, 1947.

believer in the synthesis of cultures. He was proud to think of the racial mixture in India: "My remote ancestors blended with one another with the utmost freedom and we of the present generation are a result of that blend." [57] Declaring the object of the national college (Gujarat Vidyapith) started under his inspiration he expressed his own ideal thus:

> The (Gujarat) Vidyapith does not propose to feed on, or re-peat, the ancient cultures. It rather hopes to build a new culture based on the traditions of the past and enriched by the experience of later times. It stands for synthesis of the different cultures that have come to stay in India, that have influenced Indian life, and that, in their turn, have themselves been influenced by the spirit of the soil.[58]

Gandhi's whole theory of education was fundamentally based on his deep conviction that truth and love are the most abiding bases of human society and the individual's progress. Every person should be physically, mentally, and spiritually educated to realize truth and love in every sphere of life, so that the individual, society, and humanity can progress towards increasing happiness. He did think neither that everything ancient or Indian was good, nor that everything that is modern is good. On the contrary he believed in the necessity of study, research, and experiment, without bias, to discover truth from all sources, ancient and modern, Eastern and Western. He believed also in the necessity of the experimental application of the highest moral principles to the planning of society, government, and political relations in international life. Gandhi's whole life was an example of this faith.

57. *BSG*, p. 298.
58. *Ibid.*

MEN AND WOMEN IN SOCIETY

Gandhi's conception of the relative positions of men and women in society should be briefly mentioned here. His individualism followed the theory of the *Gita* that every person can attain the highest good by recognizing realistically his or her own inherent nature, aptitude, position, and by performing the duties of the station determined by these undeniable factors. So Gandhi desired that a man should be a good *man*, and a woman should be a good *woman*, each developing in his and her own way. Man is equipped by nature to support and protect the family, and a woman is equipped by nature to play the role of a mother and caretaker of the children and the home. "Each is a complement of the other. The one cannot live without the other's active help." The work of each is essential and valuable for human existence and should be treated as a sacred and honorable duty.

Gandhi strongly disapproved, therefore, the modern tendency in women to imitate men and to do the work of men almost in every sphere. This is a sad confusion of ideals and is bound to create chaos in society. He realizes however that man's unjust attempt to domineer over women is largely responsible for the creation of an "inferiority complex" in women and this bad reaction. Man should respect woman's part in life and she should carry on her own duties with a sense of dignity. If the mother does not play her part, man will disappear from existence. "There is as much bravery in keeping one's home in good order and condition as there is in defending it against attack from without."

But, on the other hand, it is possible to exaggerate the distinction between man and woman and ignore their fundamental spiritual unity. "The soul in both is the same. The two live the same life, have the same feelings." So Gandhi concludes, "The division of the spheres of work being recognized, the general qualities and culture required are practically the same for both the sexes." [59] Gandhi was a great advocate of equality of the two in educational, civic, and spiritual matters. He devoted a good part of his life to the removal of many Indian customs that cramped the full development of womanhood. He even encouraged those women who would accept an unattached life of strict celibacy to be able to devote themselves wholly to social service. The heroic parts played by women for the political emancipation of India as followers and associates of Gandhi were the rewards of his service in the interest of women. That Indian women, within such a short time, could outshine their sisters in other countries by successfully occupying the posts of a cabinet minister, an ambassador, a governor, and the like in free India, would also show that women can rise to eminent heights in public life.

But in spite of all these Gandhi believed that for the general run of men and women, married life with a spiritual direction is the ideal thing. He says, "It is no doubt an excellent thing for girls to remain unmarried for the sake of service, but the fact is that only one in a million is able to do so." [60] There was a time when Gandhi was believed to advocate celibacy as a general idea, and marriage as a concession to the weak. He no doubt preferred celibacy for devoted and whole-time social workers. But experience

59. *Ibid.*, p. 272.
60. *H*, March 22, 1942.

taught him gradually the difficulty as well as the undesirability of this ideal for the common man and woman. As a votary of truth he expresses his mature view in the *Harijan* (March 22, 1942) very clearly as follows:

> *Marriage is a natural thing* in life, and to consider it derogatory in any sense is *wholly wrong*. When one imagines any act a fall, it is difficult, however hard one tries, to raise oneself. The ideal is to look upon marriage as a sacrament and therefore to *lead a life of self-restraint in the married estate*. Marriage in Hinduism is one of the four ashramas. In fact the other three are based on it.[61]

This maturer view of Gandhi's makes him almost echo the standard Hindu ideal as taught by Manu, rather than the extreme ascetic ideal of the Jaina and the Buddhist monks.

"The ideal that marriage aims at," says Gandhi, "is that of spiritual union through the physical. The human love that it incarnates is intended to serve as a stepping stone to divine or universal love." [62] This is the ideal, we saw, that Gandhi practised in his life. He had infinite faith in the inner goodness of every man and woman, and he sincerely believed that what he, starting as an ordinary person of lust, could achieve everyone else could also achieve. He had particular faith in the capacity of women to resist lust. His constant appeal was, therefore, to woman to help man overcome his weakness and turn the relation of flesh to that of a spiritual union, to a life of comradeship in the search of truth and the practice of universal love.

For such an ideal life Gandhi, like Manu, tries to impress that the object of sexual relation should be nothing but get-

61. *Ibid.* (our italics).
62. *BSG*, p. 273.

ting a child, which is nature's intention too. Therefore, every couple should develop a keen sense of responsibility about sex-relation, the full implication, economic and otherwise, of begetting a child. The cultivation of such a consciousness of moral and economic responsibility will naturally lead to self-restraint. It will prevent indulgence for the sake of mere pleasure which degrades individuals and society. Slavery to passions makes moral and spiritual progress impossible.

Gandhi strongly disapproves the modern tendencies and customs growing in India and the West to rouse and appeal to sex instincts through literature, pictures, music, dresses, and other innumerable ways. All these spell the signs of decadence though they pass in the name of modernism and civilization. He particularly regrets to see through all these the work of sex-appetite that reduces a woman to the mere object of lust. A civilization that treats any person, man or woman, as an object of lust, degrades the individual to a mere tool. It is doomed to ruin. History told Gandhi of the ruin of individuals and nations that became slaves to passions. Here again Gandhi believes that it is woman who can become the leader and savior. For, he thinks that it is man who is more often the tempter and aggressor. Woman, as mother, shows infinite capacity for genuine love and sacrifice. He says, therefore, "I have hugged the hope that in this woman will be the unquestioned leader." . . . "Let her transfer that love to the whole of humanity, let her forget that she ever was or can be the object of man's lust. And she will occupy her proud position by the side of man as his mother, maker and silent leader." [63] It should only be added that

63. *Ibid.*, pp. 272–73.

Mrs. Gandhi was the concrete background of these beliefs and hopes.

POLITICS

Though Gandhi became a world figure in politics, the roots of his existence lay in his moral and religious life. With his insatiable love of humanity and the philosophy of life as "one indivisible whole" he was irresistibly drawn into politics primarily to help more than three-hundred million enslaved fellow countrymen out of misery. Political work for him was the service of God in men, without which he could not emancipate himself from the bonds of selfishness nor realize God. As he puts it:

I count no sacrifice too great for the sake of seeing God face to face. The whole of my activity whether it may be called social, political, humanitarian or ethical is directed to that end. And as I know that God is found more often in the lowliest. . . . Hence my passion for the service of the suppressed classes. And as I cannot render this service without entering politics, I find myself in them. . . . I am but a struggling . . . servant of India and therethrough, of humanity.[64]

Politics have been generally regarded in every country as the sphere of human life where the ordinary laws of morality do not apply. In most political dealings, either of the rulers with the ruled, or of the subjects with the rulers, or of one country with another, tact and success have always taken the foremost place. Secrecy, deception, cunning, the fomenting of quarrels, exploitation of differences, ruling by division, and the like are all fair in politics, only if they succeed. This has been particularly true in international polit-

64. *Ibid.*, p. 45.

ical dealings, since morality has primarily been regarded as a thing to be practised within the same social or national group. The killing of the enemy of the country has invariably been applauded as a duty worthy of the highest national honors.

Gandhi's great mission in life was to revolutionize politics by ethics. Through a series of experiences and experiments in private and public life Gandhi became more and more convinced that the problems that face humanity in different spheres of human relation, private and public, could be more effectively and permanently solved by applying the moral principles of truth and love.

Gandhi applied to politics the teachings of Buddha and Christ: "Conquer hate by love, untruth by truth, violence by suffering." [65] The practice of this principle is based on "an implicit trust in human nature," that is to say, on the firm belief that deep down in man, however bad he may appear to be, there is the God in him, that is, there is reason in him that responds to truthful behavior and there is love in him that can be aroused by love and sympathy. The more we distrust any man, in private and public life, the more we debase him and ourselves. Distrust creates greater distrust and deceitfulness; hate brings greater hatred, violence greater violence. Immorality and suffering continue to increase all around, and the world becomes a hell. On the other hand, trust in the inner goodness of man evokes truthful and candid behavior, love dissolves hatred, fear, and violence. Even though this ideal of perfect behavior cannot be fully reached the more we can practise it, the more does private and public life become free from conflict, blessed and happy.

Gandhi practised this method, first in South Africa, under

65. *Ibid.*, p. 220.

the inspiration of Tolstoy who advocated nonresistance of evil based on soul-force or love-force. It was then known as the Passive Resistance movement. The discriminatory "Asiatic Act" in the Transvaal "had to go before this mighty force." Gandhi repeated the same method in India to remove many minor and major bad state laws, social customs, and practices, and finally to remove British rule from India by the accumulated force of his movements led for about thirty years.

With growing experience Gandhi discovered the defects and pitfalls that the method might involve, the bad reactions it might create, the mental and moral preparation necessary for the followers, and the environmental conditions necessary for its successful application. He regarded this long experience as a series of scientific experiments with soul-force or truth-force. He was humble enough to admit again and again his mistakes and imperfections. His constant appeal was to this scientific age which should seriously take up these experiments and perfect the method of its application in different spheres. He always regretted that although so much time, energy, and money were spent to discover the truths and forces of nature, yet so little was done by practical experiments to discover truths about the use of the forces of truthfulness and love, by which forces alone human society can survive and progress.

SATYAGRAHA AS A POLITICAL WEAPON

The name "passive resistance" which Gandhi adopted for his method was finally named by him *satyagraha*. This word was coined by him out of two Sanskrit words, *Satya* (truth, right) and *agraha* (firmness, determination). This change was thought necessary because "passive resistance" was found to be too narrowly construed as a weapon of the weak and it could admit of inner hatred that could ultimately even lead to violence.[66] *Satyagraha*, on the other hand, directly suggested that the method was one of strong determination to stick to what was true and right at all costs and sacrifice. And as love, according to Gandhi, was the means of realizing truth, *Satyagraha* also carried for him the implication of the method of love. While "passive resistance" suggested something negative; *Satyagraha* suggested "the active principle of love."

Consistent with this basic principle, *Satyagraha* can assume various forms according to different situations, such as: civil disobedience, that is, disobeying some bad law, non-payment of unjustifiable taxes, rents, etc.; non-cooperation or withdrawal of all help and service from the unjust aggressor; closing down of all business as a mark of protest and disapproval; hunger strike or resorting to hunger to rouse good sense; and so on. Gandhi and his followers used all these methods at different times to redress different kinds of wrongs.

But as the object of all these methods is to awaken through love the sense of justice in the wrongdoer, the person who would adopt them must first of all dispassionately inquire into the truth of the grievances and the rightness of the course of action adopted and of the redress demanded. He must purify himself by removing violence from thought, speech,

66. See *Autobiography*, Part IV, Chap. XXVI.

and action. He must be prepared to sacrifice everything including life if the wrongdoer resorts to violence to stop the nonviolent struggle.

It would be found, therefore, that such a method can be adopted only by persons who are selfless, fearless, self-controlled, morally pure, and have belief in the inner goodness of human nature. Moral preparation is the essential thing in this method. One who is not himself truthful, just, and free from hatred cannot arouse any sense of justice or sympathy in others. *Satyagraha* is not, again, meant for the weak; it is for those who have the highest kind of courage, and who can face cheerfully, and without the slightest inclination to retaliate, "bullets, bayonets or even slow death by torture."

Satyagraha is not to be resorted to frivolously. "Since *satyagraha* is one of the most powerful methods of direct action, a *satyagrahi* exhausts all other means before he resorts to *satyagraha*." [67] He explains his just grievances coolly and calmly to the public and the aggressor, appeals to his reason, gives him time to think, and if even then the latter does not agree to rectify the wrong, the *satyagrahi* gives him due notice of his intention to launch the nonviolent movement and then actually does so. He avoids "opportunism, camouflage or patched up compromises," but is always eager to come to a real understanding if he notices in the adversary any sign of repentance or "change of heart" which is the real object of this moral struggle. He never tries to humiliate the adversary. "It is never the intention of a *satyagrahi* to embarrass the wrongdoer. The appeal is never to his fear." [68] The "motto must ever be conversion by gen-

67. *YI*, October 20, 1927.
68. *H*, March 25, 1939.

tle persuasion and a constant appeal to the head and the heart." [69]

But it may be asked if there is really the God in man in the form of reason, appeal to reason by argument, debate, and conference should be enough to rouse his good sense. Why should there be any need for the *satyagrahi's* voluntary suffering. Gandhi replies: "I have found that mere appeal to reason does not answer where prejudices are agelong. . . . Reason has to be strengthened by suffering and suffering opens the eyes of understanding." [70] Suffering, on the one hand, acts as a self-test to the moral fighter; if his issue is not genuine and right he would not be prepared to suffer for it. On the other hand, suffering shows to the wrongdoer also that there must be some genuine cause for grievance requiring urgent attention.

The Advantage of Nonviolent Fight

The adoption of this method of love has various advantages. While every violent fight leaves behind some bitterness and cause for future dispute, this moral method ends in reconciliation and removal of bitterness. It ennobles the wrongdoer by changing his heart and it strengthens the moral qualities of the fighter. In fact Gandhi demands that before fighting with the wrongdoer one should analyse one's own heart and behavior and try to find out his own faults, defects and weaknesses that tempt wrongdoers and create enemies. A man is his own worst foe, but he can also be his own best friend, says the *Gita*. He befriends himself and

69. *BSG*, p. 222.
70. *YI*, March 19, 1925.

others when he reforms himself from within and removes the defects that gave a loophole to the enemy.

The greatest advantage of a nonviolent fight is that it places the wrongdoer between the two horns of a dilemma. If he tries to suppress the nonviolent agitation of the oppressed by violence, by beating, shooting, and killing the latter, he gradually loses the moral support of the neutral world at large whose sympathy goes out to the nonretaliating oppressed people and strengthens them. If on the other hand the wrongdoer does not suppress the agitation, then also it gains greater strength every day until the wrong is removed. This was verified by the many nonviolent struggles Gandhi led in South Africa and India for more than forty years.

Gandhi adopted this method of self-purifying nonviolent fight against all cases of injustice, tyranny, and oppression. He adopted it in all political struggles for ousting the British rule from India. He would call his oppressed countrymen to search their own hearts and purify themselves and the country of all major social, economic, and moral evils which had weakened and degraded the people and which made them the easy victims of exploitation and oppression. During the long years of Gandhian leadership in India, political movement resolved itself, therefore, along different paths of social, economic, educational, and moral reformation and reconstruction. Constructive work went on side by side with political agitation. Gandhi's constant advice was: "Exploitation thrives on our sins. Remove the sins and exploitation will stop. Rather than blaming the British blame yourself and purify yourself. Hate not the British but the British system."

The more Gandhi succeeded in training up nonviolent soldiers in his various struggles and the more they could suffer the violent attempts of the opponents to stop the non-violent movements, the more did people become attracted to join his ranks and fight his cause. Sometimes Gandhi started a campaign such as civil disobedience (that is, break-ing a certain bad law) with a handful of followers. When these were sent to prison or battered or shot, hundreds were roused into sympathy and flocked in to take their places. The spirit of nonviolent suffering became contagious. Thou-sands took the places of the persecuted hundreds and so on until the whole country threw itself into the fight. The prisons, guns, bullets, and soldiers became all too few for the entire disaffected population. The rulers were over-whelmed by the results of their violent methods and came to terms for which Gandhi was always prepared. For he bore neither any spite, nor any false sense of personal prestige. "Change of heart" in the adversary was his objective and whenever he saw any sign of that, he would even risk being fooled and deceived and would call off the struggle. For it was Gandhi's belief that the deceiver would be ultimately deceived. His long life of varied experience justified this belief.

On the other hand, whenever Gandhi saw that his fol-lowers were growing violent, he would try his hardest to control them. If necessary, he would stop the movement and retire into silence to check what defects there were in himself and his lieutenants. Often he would even go on a long fast to purify himself and to rouse the followers to a sense of repentance for their violence and lapses.

THE GENUINE FEW CAN LEAD

Inward strength—an unflinching faith in God or in the inner goodness of man, and a determination to stick to truth and love—was regarded by Gandhi as the true source of strength in a moral fight. "The puniest individual may have a stout heart," and he may make the ideal soldier and leader. Number also does not count much. "Strength of numbers is the delight of the timid. The valiant in spirit glory in fighting alone." . . . "The best and the most solid work was done in the wilderness of minority." . . . "Take the great prophets, Zoroaster, Buddha, Jesus, Mohammed—they all stood alone." [71] If the ideal be pure, if it be based on truth and love, it will gradually gather force and followers, and it will strengthen a good movement, whether social or political.

But it is very important to remember that the conversion of others by the method of truth and love may take a long time, as all methods of abiding value do. It is only by living up to one's high ideals and serving humanity in their light for a long time that one can inspire genuine confidence, attract love, and expect to influence others. Again, real leadership and influence come unsought. One who is ardently engaged in perfecting himself, unconsciously reforms others around him and becomes an uncrowned king of their hearts. It is by spontaneous "self-giving," as Rabindranath Tagore used to say, that Gandhi captured the hearts of the people.

71. See *BSG*, pp. 241-45.

POLITICAL FREEDOM

Though the achievement of political freedom was the immediate and ostensible goal of Gandhi's movement in India, it was to him only a means to a higher end, namely, spiritual freedom. The word which he, along with others, used for self-rule is *svaraj,* a word which is used in the early philosophical literature of India, such as the Upanishads, to connote "One who rules himself," that is, one who is spiritually free.

Life and Reality are both indivisible. Life cannot progress in part. Social, economic, political, and moral freedoms are intimately interlocked and interdependent. There must be all-sided development. Spiritual well-being consists in the realization of Reality in its entirety. It needs an integral progress of all sides of human life. "On the principle that the greater includes the less," says Gandhi, "national independence or material freedom is included in the spiritual." [72] India's loss of political freedom made economic exploitation and poverty irremediable. Social and moral degradation followed in their wake and reacted on them again. There was a vicious circle of mutually caused and enhanced miseries of all kinds. There was thus a total spiritual degradation. Without political recovery, the other aspects of the nation's life could not be improved. No spiritual progress was possible for the country.

Political freedom thus appeared to Gandhi to be as necessary a part of spiritual freedom as the health of one vital

72. *YI,* March 20, 1930.

part of the body, like the heart or liver, is for the well-being of the entire body. Gandhi did not, therefore, believe in cloistered religion: "I do not believe that the spiritual law works on a field of its own. On the contrary, it expresses itself only through the ordinary activities of life. It thus affects the economic, the social and the political fields." [73]

Gandhi toiled the whole of his life in each of these fields to realize God through the service of his creation. "Man's ultimate aim is the realization of God. . . . This can only be done by service of all. . . . I cannot find him apart from humanity." [74]

Just because Gandhi treated political activity as a means to a higher purpose, he never lost the sense of direction in the midst of the bitterest political struggles and controversies. His wider and steady vision helped him keep his temper cool and judgment clear; and he never lost his sense of humor. An English professor from Oxford who had the opportunity of observing Gandhi in England being "sifted and cross-questioned" by a group of eminent English leaders for three hours observed: "The conviction came to me, that not since Socrates has the world seen his equal for absolute self-control and composure." [75]

THE STATE AND THE INDIVIDUAL

Gandhi regarded the individual as the center of authority and value. The state and government derive their existence and power from the individuals. Their object should, there-

73. *Ibid.*, September 3, 1925.
74. *BSG*, p. 25.
75. Sarvepalli Radhakrishnan, *Mahatma Gandhi* (London: G. Allen & Unwin, Ltd., 1949), p. 291.

fore, be to help the all-round evolution of the individual by enacting and enforcing laws, preventing exploitation, ensuring security, peace and the progress of individuals. The state should always preserve the spirit of service and should never behave like the master of the people.

The people should always remember that the state or government cannot exist for a moment without their cooperation. This idea should guide the people both positively and negatively. For the people should cooperate to their utmost with the state in all its welfare works, in preserving all good laws, and in defending the country at the cost of their lives. In doing all this, the people advance their own ultimate good. In learning to sacrifice their pleasures and comforts for the sake of other fellow creatures, individuals only expand their own selves and advance towards the realization of themselves and God.

But, on the other hand, when the state begins to exploit the people and hinder their progress, it is the sacred duty of the people to withdraw their cooperation from the state and reform the state by moral pressure—by nonviolent noncooperation which Gandhi adopted for paralyzing the British Government in India.

The edge of political consciousness should, therefore, always be kept sharp, and the state and government of the people should be kept straight by the judicious operation of the two principles of cooperation and non-cooperation. As for the individual's moral life, so also for the state, "Eternal vigilance is the price of liberty." Gandhi says: "Self-government depends entirely upon our internal strength; upon our ability to fight against the heaviest odds. Indeed, self-government which does not require that *continuous*

striving to attain it and to sustain it, is not worth the name." [76]
Gandhi was bitterly conscious of the fact that like a foreign government, even a national government might become an obstacle to the freedom and growth of the individual. He saw how in many so-called free countries the individuals were sacrificed to the whims of the state and the dictators. He did not like, therefore, the authority of the state to be so rigid and absolute as to smother the conscience and the moral growth of the individual. Gandhi strongly asserts: *"The individual is the one supreme consideration. . . . * I look upon an increase of the power of the state with the greatest fear, because, although while apparently doing good by minimizing exploitation, it does the greatest harm to mankind by destroying *individuality which lies at the root of all progress.*" [77]

The state at present no doubt has to be armed with power, munitions and soldiers for the protection of the people and the maintenance of peace and order. But it is a bad day for the individuals when they leave the initiative to the state, and passively look to it for everything being done. Such implicit dependence on the state gradually leads it to autocracy and dictatorship. Individuals should themselves constantly strive, and mutually help one another, to discipline themselves morally, so that gradually they become law unto themselves and require less and less force to behave under the external pressure of the laws of the state. The state should also gradually become a welfare institution, and less and less coercive. Speaking of this ideal state Gandhi says:

76. *BSG*, p. 35 (our italics).
77. *Ibid.*, p. 26 (our italics), and *BMR*, p. 413.

"There is then a state of enlightened anarchy. In such a state every one is his own ruler. He rules himself in such a manner that he is never a hindrance to his neighbour. . . . But the ideal is never fully realized in life. Hence the classical statement of Thoreau that that Government is best which governs the least." [78]

For economic organization, too, Gandhi was in favor of private enterprise, and of encouraging the individual to develop industries and business along altruistic lines. He envisaged, of course, the necessity of the state's checking exploitation and running a limited number of industries. But he was strongly opposed to the forcible liquidation of capitalists by the state.

He expresses his opinion on the matter thus:

It is my firm conviction that if the state suppressed capitalism by violence, it will be caught in the coils of violence itself and fail to develop non-violence at any time.

What I would personally prefer, would be, not a centralization of power in the hands of the state but an extension of the sense of trusteeship; as in my opinion, the violence of private ownership is less injurious than the violence of the state. However, if it is unavoidable, I would support a minimum of state-ownership.[79]

Without moral discipline, moral persuasion and voluntary control of the greed for wealth and power, neither the individual nor society can prosper. Man's creation of a strong state-mechanism to check forcibly dishonest tendencies in society has led to many abuses. Again and again his own creation has prevented him from rising to his full stature.

78. *BSG*, p. 40.
79. *BMR*, p. 412.

140 *The Philosophy of Mahatma Gandhi*

THE SPIRIT OF TRUE DEMOCRACY

True democracy can never be based on violence and force. In order to promote the full and free growth of the individual, a democratic society must be based on fellow-feeling, reasonable understanding, mutual trust and cooperation. It is on such principles that humanity has so far progressed and it is on them again that mankind can progress still further. The main principle of human love has always inspired man to seek the good of self in the good of all. To the extent that this principle has been followed there has been peace among men and men, groups and groups, nations and nations. This principle of love or nonviolence should be the basis of every human organization from the smallest unit called the family to the largest organization, the international human family. If any of these component units be immoral, that is, be based on violence, hatred, greed, and the like, the character of the larger whole will be vitiated and spoiled by strife, war, and ruin. The peace or happiness of mankind will necessarily be endangered.

Democracy can grow only by the voluntary efforts of the individual and it cannot be enforced from outside. Gandhi says: "I hold that democracy cannot be evolved by forcible methods. The spirit of democracy cannot be imposed from without. It has to come from within." [80] The good individual is, therefore, the essential requisite of a good democracy. The five-fold moral ideals previously discussed can assure both the progress of the individual and the evolution of ideal democracy.

80. Pattabhi Sitaramaiyya, *The History of the Indian National Congress* (Allahabad, 1935), p. 982.

IDEAL GOVERNMENT

Gandhi spent his life in leading his country to freedom. Though he expressed his ideas about an ideal democratic government from time to time, he did not think it either opportune or necessary to formulate in concrete detail the nature of an ideal government. In fact his idea was that if the means was sound, the end must be good. So he busied himself mostly in forging a nonviolent means for the emancipation of his country. Moreover as the nature of a democratic government should be determined by the liberated people, he did not like to dictate in advance the form of government India should have. We can mention however a few things which he considered essential.

Gandhi did not attach much importance to the name by which an ideal government should be called. He observed in contemporary politics many misleading names. He also learned from past Indian history that the rule of even monarchs and emperors like Rama and Ashoka could achieve high ideals. The things he prized most were (1) all-sided welfare of the people which was traditionally associated with the rule of Rama, (2) government based on nonviolence and moral enthusiasm, associated with Emperor Ashoka, (3) and, as a corollary to this, nonexploitation of either any class or any country outside one's own.

But Gandhi was aware that the thought of a benevolent monarchy was out of tune with the age. He, therefore, wanted for India *svaraj* or self-rule, by which he meant government "by the consent of the people as ascertained by the largest number of the adult population, male and female, native born or domiciled." [81] He also wanted that the people should not "act like sheep"; that they should take an active part in determining their own form of government in accordance with "the genius" of the people. Self-rule should be "sovereignty of the people based on pure moral authority." [82]

Though Gandhi realized that in popular government the majority view has to be the basis of practical action, he was anxious to point out:

> The rule of majority has a narrow application, i.e., one should yield to the majority in matters of detail. But it is slavery to be amenable to the majority, no matter what its decisions are. . . . Under democracy individual liberty of opinion and action is jealously guarded. . . . What we want, I hope, is a government not based on coercion even of a minority but on its conversion. [83]

This note sounded by Gandhi would suggest that in a good democracy the majority should be democratic enough to see, with sympathy, that the minority's interests do not suffer and on the other hand, that the minority should be bold enough to stand up for their legitimate moral aspirations and should fight for them in the nonviolent ways previously discussed.

But Gandhi believed that the individuals and minorities were apt to be ignored and neglected in huge representative systems of government. He was strongly in favor, therefore, of a federation of decentralized units of ideal village republics. Each village should be self-contained so far as possible in respect to food, clothes, water supply, milk supply, sanita-

81. *YI*, January 29, 1925.
82. *BSG*, p. 115.
83. *YI*, March 2, 1922, and December 19, 1929.

tion, education up to a secondary standard, recreation, for children and adults, etc. Every activity should be conducted on the cooperative basis, as far as possible. "Non-violence with its technique of *satyagraha* and non-cooperation will be the sanction of the village community." The villagers will guard the village by rotation. "The Government of the village will be conducted by the *Panchayat* of five persons, annually elected by adult villagers, male and female. . . . This *Panchayat* will be the legislature, judiciary, and executive combined." [84]

In such a village republic Gandhi sees "perfect democracy based upon individual freedom. The individual is the architect of his own government. The law of non-violence rules him and his government." [85] The basic material needs of the individual being satisfied, he would be free to pursue the ideal of plain living and high thinking and work for his spiritual unfoldment. As such a village will not have accumulated surplus wealth, nor have evil intentions against others, it can hope to live in far greater peace which is necessary for moral or spiritual development.

NATIONALISM AND INTERNATIONALISM

But though Gandhi strongly advocated such village republics as conducive to the development of the ideal individual he believed, on the other hand, in the necessity of mutual dependence in certain matters, economic and cultural. In fact he believed that when the individual developed fully, in the favorable atmosphere of the village, a strong

84. *BSG*, p. 74.
85. *Ibid.*

moral and social sense, he would develop also a love for humanity which would break all national and geographical barriers. As we saw previously he, like the other great thinkers of modern India, believed that "No culture can live, if it attempts to be exclusive." He positively desired a cultural synthesis for the improvement of every culture. For example, speaking about sanitation he says, "The one thing which we can and must learn from the West is the science of municipal sanitation. . . . And as my patriotism is inclusive and admits of no enmity or ill will, I do not hesitate, in spite of my horror of Western materialism, to take from the West what is beneficial for me." [86]

It would appear from this that Gandhi's ideal of nationalism and patriotism were not exclusive. Indian nationalism drew its inspiration from the dominant Indian belief in the fundamental unity of humanity in spite of its diversity, and the consequent belief in the reasonableness of human equality. So nationalism logically led on to internationalism. Love of man impelled Gandhi to be both a nationalist and an internationalist. He wanted to effect the political recovery of India not by appealing to racial or class hatred, but to the spirit of truth and love.

So Gandhi says: "My notion of *Purna* Swaraj (i.e. complete self-rule) is not isolated independence but healthy and dignified interdependence." Again, "Our nationalism can be no peril to other nations inasmuch as we will exploit none just as we will allow none to exploit us. Through swaraj *we would serve the whole world*." [87]

Gandhi vividly depicted his dream of the gradual spiritual

86. *Ibid.*, p. 299.
87. *Ibid.*, pp. 118 f. (our italics).

expansion of the individual towards its identity with humanity through service and self-sacrifice, in the following memorable passage published in his weekly, *Young India* (Sept. 17, 1925), while he was bitterly struggling against British rule and was being imprisoned and punished again and again: "I would like to see India free and strong so that she may offer herself as a *willing* and *pure* sacrifice *for the betterment of the world.* The individual, being free, sacrifices himself to the family, the latter for the village, the village for the district, the district for the province, the province for the nation, the nation for all."

So politics could become Gandhi's lifelong religion, nationalism the step to internationalism.

4

Moral Leadership of the World

> If we are to make progress, we must not repeat
> history but make new history. We must add to the
> inheritance left by our ancestors. If we may make
> new discoveries and inventions in the phenomenal
> world, must we declare our bankruptcy in the
> spiritual domain? Is it impossible to multiply the
> exceptions so as to make them the rule? Must
> man always be brute first and man after, if at all?
> —*Young India*, May 6, 1926

The brief account of the life and philosophy of Mahatma
Gandhi would show that his long life of seventy-nine years
was a series of experiments in the spiritual domain. The con-
sensus of contemporary thought has placed Gandhi among
the greatest men of all times, not because he was the originator of any new principle, but because he demonstrated in
practical politics the applicability of the moral ideas of the
great world teachers of the past.

The experiments of Gandhi were, as we have seen, con-

ducted with nearly four hundred million people in South
Africa and India and for half a century. Gandhi always behaved like a humble seeker after truth and as an experimenter
in an untrodden field. He was modest enough to acknowl-
edge that his achievements fell far short of his ideals. But
the success he repeatedly won in many fields in his nonviolent struggles against personal, social, and political evils
aroused great hopes in himself and other thoughtful persons
in all parts of the world, among whom are to be found even
some great British statesmen who were once the opponents
of Gandhi's movements.[1]

The world has been passing now through the aftereffects
of the two great world wars which have revealed the brute
in man and shaken all confidence in his inner goodness. Even
the most civilized peoples are being irresistibly led by the
violent methods of stopping war into more wars and the perpetration of acts which outrage their long cherished ideals.
The world is being caught up again in a long and grim cold
war for which even the most pacifist nations are engaged in
coolly devising the most powerful instruments for the destruction of fellow beings. Today even democratic govern-
ments are being unconsciously led to adopt autocratic methods for saving democracy. The long-taxed civil population,
the orphans, the widows, the displaced, the bereaved, and
the molested in every country shudder now at the very
thought of another war.

Gandhi's experiments in nonviolent ways of life acquire
special importance at this critical moment and call for further trial and application. As a sincere and humble votary

1. See Sarvepalli Radhakrishnan, *Mahatma Gandhi* (London: G. Allen
& Unwin, Ltd., 1949), containing about 100 essays by eminent persons of
the world on Gandhi's life and work.

of truth, Gandhi always appealed to fellow-seekers of truth in other places to try the nonviolent methods for the solution of their problems and to evolve thereby more effective methods suiting the geniuses of their own peoples and their own conditions.

Gandhi's great regret was that while so much human energy, time, and money were being devoted to the discovery of the truths of outer nature, so little was being done to reveal and utilize the deeper truths of human nature. Even the most advanced peoples blindly assume the truth of the brute in man, plan human relations on this crude basis, and then apply all scientific talents to the perfection of destructive implements that can take care of the brute, by threat and violence. In this process of killing the brute in the enemy by violence, man turns both himself and his enemy into greater brutes.

It has been seen in the course of the preceding pages that Gandhi's social and political experiments are all based on the recognition of the moral foundation of human nature and human society. Human progress can be assured only if the life of the individual, society, country, and the world as a whole be more and more based on the fundamental moral principles of truthfulness, nonviolence, nonstealing, self-control, and nonpossession. The regeneration of moral life requires, as Gandhi tried to show, the progressive replanning of social, economic, and political life on these moral principles. The raising of the standard of living has become today the slogan of the West and also of the East. But though economic progress is essential for man, it is not all that is needed. One-sided stress on economic ideals leads the world to greater strife and misery. "That economics is untrue," says Gandhi, "which ignores or disregards moral values."

Even a cursory glance at modern life, in its different spheres will show how the modern world is gradually getting into a hopeless morass by the violation of the basic moral principles; and how the successive wars have been impairing the moral foundations of human society everywhere.

The growing disregard for truthfulness is most evident today in commercial life where blatant self-advertisement has reduced all superlatives to competitive lies and howling falsehoods. Modern publicity, for both civil and military purposes, has been perfecting, with the help of up-to-date psychological researches, the art of "cooking up" selected half-truths and wishful thoughts into an attractive kind of specious truths to delude the unwary. The bitter nemesis of such unscrupulous methods is that even plain, honest truth has become suspect in the modern world. It is an undeniable fact that even the pledged word of a great political authority of today does not command the trust that the word of a simple illiterate villager used to do in primitive days. How can there be national or international understanding in a world of growing falsehood and distrust?

The evils of violence in the modern world are too patent to require special mention. It is, however, necessary to point out a few peculiar, disturbing phenomena. The biggest cities of the world, created by the centralization of power and large-scale industries and commerce, have developed equally big centers of crime and underworlds that use the most up-to-date scientific devices for the perpetration of crimes defying all civil authorities. But what is proving most disconcerting to society is the recent tendency of the molestation of innocent children, men, and women by the scientifically

equipped gangs of teen-agers [2] born and bred in the pro-
tracted demoralizing atmosphere of the last world war which
completely let loose all the violent impulses of the entire
human race. It may be relevant to remember that the Hitler
movement in Germany started first with the organization
of youngsters demoralized by the aftereffects of the first
world war. In the field of modern scientific warfare (as con-
trasted with the hand-to-hand fight of ancient days) the
most dangerous development is that a fighter can just press
a button somewhere *without any violent feeling* and without
realizing vividly the huge destruction of life and property
his simple act has produced somewhere else.

Exploitation of groups by groups, and countries by countries is the manifestation of the violation of the moral principle of nonstealing as interpreted by Gandhi. The maldistribution of wealth created by exploitation is the parent of
most of the political rivalries and revolutions that have been
rocking the modern world and violently pushing it towards
greater equalization of wealth. It has become the greatest
menace to free enterprise. Nor can this stop so long as free
enterprise means freedom to make money just as one pleases.

The lack of the practice of "nonpossession" or voluntary
renunciation of superfluous wealth in societies which favor
free enterprise is creating growing inequalities and the consequent demand of the poorer classes for all kinds of artificial
state controls and even for the complete socialization of all
sources of wealth. Corruption in public life, amongst even

2. See Howard Whitman, *Terror in the Streets* (New York: Dial
Press, 1951), and "On Growing Youth Delinquency," *New York Times*,
April 20, 1951.

the highest officials, is another hideous manifestation of the uncontrolled greed for possession.

The want of self-control, in general, and continence, in particular, is becoming growingly evident in modern life, in every part of the world, in the many morbid phenomena of social decadence. Uncontrolled indulgence in stimulants and narcotics, careless abandon to thrills and sensations, lustful appeal to sex instincts, promiscuous relations of the sexes, and the like, have been manifesting themselves in the modern ways of life, in art and literature. What is still worse, these are often rationalized and justified on the basis of some half-assimilated hypotheses of abnormal psychology and flaunted as the marks of modernism and progress. But their disastrous effects are unmistakably pronounced by the increasing incidence of neuroses, frustration, broken homes, unwed motherhood, and other sad tales with which modern society abounds.

In all these morbid phenomena of moral life, the East and the West are sadly following the same pattern. Overawed by the tremendous mechanical powers and material progress of the West, the East has lost confidence in its own moral and spiritual heritage, and is blindly following the West— whether it be the Eastern West or the Western West.

Depressing as the woeful tale of modern decadence is, a realistic diagnosis of the ills and a firm determination to overcome them can pave the way to recovery. It is now believed on scientific evidence that man must have lived on this earth for at least two million years. He must have also passed through and overcome many a crisis during this incredibly long period. Things which have physically and morally helped man to survive have survived and come down through the ages. The basic principles of morality found in all human societies and religions of the world are some of those precious principles which have unified man and saved him from vices by which he could perish. Man can survive also the crises of the modern times by a determined effort to practise those moral ideals in every sphere of life.

It will be heartening to remember that the ethical and spiritual springs of human life have not yet been completely dried up. It is they that have been preventing total disruption of society and destruction of men even under the present try ing circumstances. The present moral crisis has really originated from the many new moral problems caused by the too sudden developments of science, technology, and industrialized society, and the too sudden coming together of the different nations through rapid transportation. Humanity has not had enough time for moral adjustment to the overwhelming atmosphere of new truths about nature and mind, nor has it had time to handle with wise control the enormous physical powers achieved by technology. The present crisis is the danger signal that urgently calls for the development of moral powers commensurate with the physical and mental developments.

That the fundamental moral instincts are still active can be observed in the different private walks of life, and even in the back pages of the newspapers which often exaggerate the evils of the age by printing all social scandals on their front pages. When the stories of cruelty, corruption, and greed with large headlines seem to announce a moral chaos we can still overcome our sickness by turning to such things as the story of a boy, with the compassion of a Buddha, jumping into the icy Harlem to save a drowning dog at the risk of his own life; [3] the story of two movers of furniture finding one thousand dollars and turning it over to the police while they had only one dollar and one cent between them; [4] the story of a merchant who made a secret will thirty years ago to give away two-thirds of the profits of his business for public charity which has received 30 million dollars up till now,[5] and so on. Their number is legion; we have only to look for them. The story of Gandhi described here is also a convincing demonstration to this sceptical age that the high moral ideals of Buddha, Socrates, Christ, and other great teachers of the past can be practised in all spheres of life including the usually demoralizing field of politics. The successive efforts of the League of Nations and the United Nations organizations have also aroused hope in so far as they have been able to awaken and mobilize the moral support of different nations, avoiding the formation of power blocks based on intrigues, exploitation, and common enmity.

Man can survive only if he has faith in himself. It is by this faith and determination that Gandhi, born an ordinary man, made himself so great and became the moral leader of millions, and achieved by the methods of truth and love things which looked like miracles in the modern age. His

3. *New York Sunday News*, November 25, 1951, published the item: "Joe McLenon, 14, saw a dog swimming for life in the middle of New York City's chilly Harlem River. Joe stripped to shorts, plunged in, steered the dog to shore. Reason: Joe likes dogs."

4. *Ibid.*: "Joseph and Peter Daly, moving men: they turned over to police $1,000 they found in a sofa they were moving from a New York apartment. At the time, they had exactly $1.01 between them."

5. *New York Times*, February 18, 1952, published the story of George Robert White, late President of the Cuticura Soap Corporation, whose secret charity has been made known only now, thirty years after his death in 1922.

well-begun but unfinished work calls out to every ordinary man and woman of the world—particularly to the young people of this new world which is full of the spirit of new enterprise—to take up the moral leadership of the world. This moral leadership is not the imposition of one's will on others, but the imposition of the reign of reason and love on one's blind and selfish passions. It is a process of reforming and guiding others unconsciously while one is consciously trying to reform oneself. It is a way of life which brings increasing opportunities for perfecting oneself by the service of fellow beings. It is an eternal process of perfection which humanity has been carrying on through trials, errors, failures and victories from time immemorial. The modern generation can hasten this process if it will, and enjoy and create greater and greater peace and happiness, for itself and the future generations.